The Australian Women's Weekly

100 fabulous CHEESECAKES

Ellen Sinclair

Food Editor

Golden Press
Sydney

Contents

Making Cheesecakes

All the information you need to turn out a beautiful cheesecake is given in this book and there are one hundred fabulous recipes from which to choose

CHEESECAKE is so rich, so luscious, you need to serve it only in small slices. One cheesecake will go a long way; in an 8 or 9 in. size it will give up to 12 servings.

There are two main types of cheesecake—baked, and unbaked. The baked cheesecakes are firmer, richer and freeze well. The unbaked cheesecakes—those which set in the refrigerator—are generally lighter, more delicate in texture; because gelatine is added to give them firmness, they are not suitable for freezing.

Recipes for both types are given in this book; there are also recipes for delicious baked and unbaked slices.

And chefs at well-known restaurants have given us their cheesecake recipes that are a dessert specialty on their menus.

Packaged cream cheese is used in some recipes. Where packaged cream cheese is not indicated, bulk cream cheese can be used; push it through a fine sieve first to break up the curds and give it finer texture.

When making baked cheesecakes, cooking times should be followed carefully. Don't overcook them. At the end of the specified cooking time, the cheesecake might still appear soft in the centre; but it becomes firmer as it stands.

An overbaked cheesecake develops grainy texture; it is inclined to shrink, crack, and become dry as it cools.

If you cool the cheesecake by the following method you'll find there is very little shrinking, and the cheesecake does not fall in the centre:

When baking time is over, turn off the oven heat, leave the oven door ajar, and let the cheesecake stand undisturbed in the oven until it is quite cool. This helps to set the soft centre and prevent it falling. It will not cause overbaking. When the cheesecake is cool, refrigerate until it has set firmly.

Large cheesecakes are best if made the day before they are to be served, then refrigerated overnight; the filling sets firmly and they're easier to cut.

For a crumb crust that will hold its shape without crumbling, and cut well, the ideal proportions are half the amount of butter to the weight of biscuit crumbs. For example, a crumb crust which used 8 oz. biscuit crumbs would hold together well with 4 oz. melted butter.

The exception to this is when a biscuit which has a good proportion of butter added to it during the manufacturing process (such as shortbread biscuits) is used for the crumb crust. This type of crust needs slightly less melted butter added. Specific quantities are given in individual recipes in this book.

The recipes which use a crumb crust specify them in a particular size to hold the quantity of filling: for example, '7 in. crumb crust,' '8 in. crumb crust.'

The 7 in. crumb crust indicates a 7 in. sandwich tin with a removable base. All others are for springform pans (except where a pie plate and its size is specified).

As a general guide, we give below the various proportions of biscuit crumbs and butter needed for each size. To this can be added a little cinnamon, nutmeg, etc.

For 7 in. sandwich tin with removable base: use 6 oz. plain sweet biscuit crumbs and 3 oz. butter.

For 8 in. springform pan: use 8 oz. plain sweet biscuit crumbs and 4 oz. butter.

For 9 in. springform pan: use 10 oz. plain sweet biscuit crumbs and 5 oz. butter.

For 10 in. to 11 in. springform pan: use 12 oz. plain sweet biscuit crumbs and 6 oz. butter.

For 8 in. to 9 in. pie plate: use 6 oz. plain sweet biscuit crumbs and 3 oz. butter.

Cheesecakes are easier to turn out if you use a springform pan. These have an adjustable case with a clip at the side; the base is removable.

Springform pans can be bought in 8 in., 9 in., and 11 in. sizes. Springform pans 10 in. in size are more difficult to obtain. A 10 in. springform pan, imported, of stainless steel, is available.

The cooled cheesecake can be removed from a 7 in. sandwich tin with removable base by gently pressing base, with cake, up through ring.

How to make a perfect crumb crust

After a cheesecake has been removed from a springform pan and crumb crust neatened, let it remain on the pan base.

Simply lift it, with base, on to serving dish. (There's a possibility of the crumb crust cracking or crumbling if you try to remove cake from base.)

But if you do want to serve the cake without the base, here's a hint: Reverse the base of the springform pan before pressing in the crumb crust. It is the slight ridge on the springform base which makes it difficult to remove cheesecake. You'll now be able to take a long-bladed knife or spatula, work it gently under the crumb crust, and carefully slide the cheesecake on to serving plate.

Cut cheesecake into wedges for serving. A thin, flexible metal spatula or knife makes it easy to remove individual wedges.

Cup and Spoon Measures

The standard eight-liquid-ounce measuring cup is used for recipes in this book. All spoon measurements are level.

Cup Measures
(Using the eight-liquid-ounce cup)

1 cup flour	4 oz.
1 cup sugar (crystal or castor)	8 oz.
1 cup icing sugar (free from lumps)	5 oz.
1 cup shortening (butter, margarine, etc.)	8 oz.
1 cup honey, golden syrup, treacle	10 oz.
1 cup brown sugar (lightly packed)	6 oz.
1 cup brown sugar (firmly packed)	8 oz.
1 cup soft breadcrumbs	2 oz.
1 cup dry breadcrumbs (made from fresh breadcrumbs)	3 oz.
1 cup packet dry breadcrumbs	4 oz.
1 cup rice (uncooked)	6 oz.
1 cup rice (cooked)	5 oz.
1 cup mixed fruit or individual fruit such as sultanas, etc.	4 oz.
1 cup grated cheese	4 oz.
1 cup nuts (chopped)	4 oz.
1 cup coconut	2½ oz.

Liquid Measures
(Using the eight-liquid-ounce cup measure)

1 cup liquid	8 oz.
2½ cups liquid	20 oz. (1 pint)
1 gill liquid	5 oz. (¼ pint)

Step 1 Put biscuits into plastic bag, crush finely with rolling pin, then sift or put through fine sieve. Or, if using electric blender, break up biscuits roughly, drop into blender a few at a time.

Step 4 Stand pan on table, take a straight-sided glass, work it smoothly over base and sides. Refrigerate 1 hour to set crumbs. Pour filling in, refrigerate or bake, according to recipe.

Step 2 Add remaining ingredients to crumbs, mix well. Grease inside of pan lightly, scatter one-third of crumb mixture across base, then press on firmly with tablespoon.

Step 3 Now turn pan on its side and put large spoonfuls of crumbs in place on side; press on with back of spoon. Continue until all sides are coated with a firm, even layer of crumbs.

Step 5 Do not remove cheese cake from pan until well refrigerated, preferably overnight. Release catch at side of pan, put hand firmly underneath, then gently push base up, easing side of pan away.

Step 6 When removed from pan, neaten edge of crumb crust by pressing sharp knife gently across; work carefully to avoid cracking crust. Use pastry brush to brush off any crumbs on filling.

Baked Cheesecakes

Baked cheesecakes are the richest cheesecake type, and have delicious variations in fillings

Wonderful Basic Cheesecake

1½ lb. cream cheese
1 teaspoon vanilla
4 eggs
1 cup sugar
1 dessertspoon grated lemon rind
1 dessertspoon lemon juice
8 in. crumb crust

Press cream cheese through strainer, blend with vanilla. Beat eggs until thick, beat in sugar gradually. Continue beating while adding cheese mixture in small portions, mixing each time until smooth. Mix in lemon juice and rind.

Spread into crumb crust, bake in moderate oven 25 to 30 minutes. Cool, then refrigerate. Just before serving, top with whipped cream, sprinkle with cinnamon or nutmeg.

Apricot Swirl Cheesecake

Crumb Crust:

6 oz. shortbread biscuits
2 oz. butter

Filling:

1½ lb. packaged cream cheese
1¼ cups sugar
6 eggs, separated
½ cup plain flour
1 cup cream
1 teaspoon grated lemon rind
2 tablespoons lemon juice
1 teaspoon vanilla

Apricot Puree:

2 oz. dried apricots
½ cup sugar
1 tablespoon rum
1¼ cups lukewarm water

Crumb Crust: Crush biscuits. Combine crushed biscuits and melted butter in a bowl. Press mixture on to base of 9 in. greased springform pan.

Refrigerate until set.

Apricot puree: Soak apricots in lukewarm water 1 hour. Add sugar, and simmer very gently with liquid until tender, approximately 30 minutes. Beat well with whisk or put through sieve. Cool, add rum, stir until smooth.

Filling: Beat together cream cheese and sugar until light and fluffy. Beat in egg-yolks until just blended; stir in sifted flour, lemon rind and juice, and vanilla. Beat egg-whites until they form soft peaks; whip cream until stiff. Fold beaten egg-whites then cream into cheese mixture. Spoon ⅓ of mixture on to crumb crust; place teaspoonfuls of apricot puree at intervals over cheese mixture, using approximately half the puree mixture. Carefully pour another ⅓ of cheese mixture over and repeat apricot layer. Top with remaining cheese mixture. Cut through mixture gently to swirl puree. Stand pan on oven tray.

Bake in slow oven 1 hour. Turn off oven heat, let stand in oven 1 hour longer.

Cool, then refrigerate.

French Cheesecake

Crust:

6 oz. plain sweet biscuits
3 oz. butter

Filling:

1½ lb. packaged cream cheese
2 tablespoons self-raising flour
1 dessertspoon grated lemon rind
¾ cup sour cream
2 eggs
¾ cup sugar
¾ cup milk

Crust: Crush biscuits. Combine biscuit crumbs and melted butter. Press into base of 9 in. springform pan, refrigerate until set.

Filling: Separate eggs. Combine egg-yolks, cheese, sifted flour, lemon rind and sour cream, beat until smooth. Beat egg-whites until soft peaks form, gradually add sugar, beat until dissolved, add milk. Gradually beat into cheese mixture. Pour on to crumb crust, stand pan on baking tray. Bake in slow oven 50 to 55 minutes.

Austrian Cheesecake

Crumb Crust:

4 oz. plain sweet biscuits	1 teaspoon cinnamon
	2 oz. butter

Filling:

1 lb. packaged cream cheese	1 tablespoon lemon juice
2 eggs	½ pint sour cream
½ cup castor sugar	1 teaspoon vanilla

Crumb Crust: Crush biscuits. Combine biscuit crumbs, cinnamon and melted butter. Press over base of 8 in. springform pan.

Refrigerate until set.

Filling: Beat cream cheese until smooth. Beat eggs and three-quarters of the sugar until thick and creamy; add to cheese with lemon juice, spoon over prepared crumb crust. Stand pan on baking tray, bake in moderate oven 30 minutes. Mix together sour cream, vanilla and remaining sugar, spread carefully over cake.

Return to hot oven, bake further 10 minutes.

Almond Cheesecake

2 oz. butter	2 oz. raisins
⅓ cup castor sugar	1 dessertspoon grated lemon rind
2 eggs, separated	
1½ oz. ground almonds	¼ cup lemon juice
8 oz. packaged cream cheese	2 tablespoons cream
2 tablespoons semolina	8 in. crumb crust

Cream together butter and sugar until light and creamy. Add lightly beaten egg-yolks, ground almonds, cream cheese, semolina, chopped raisins, grated rind and lemon juice; beat well.

Fold in softly beaten egg-whites and cream. Turn into crumb crust.

Bake in moderately slow oven 50 to 60 minutes or until filling is set.

Chocolate Mint Cheesecake

3 oz. dark chocolate	pinch bicarb. soda
3 eggs	pinch salt
¾ cup sugar	1 tablespoon creme de menthe
8 oz. packaged cream cheese	extra whipped cream
¾ cup cream	8 in. crumb crust
⅓ cup plain flour	

Chop chocolate, melt over hot water, set aside. Beat eggs until light and fluffy. Add sugar gradually, beating well until thick and lemon-coloured. Beat together cream cheese and cream until smooth and thickened. Add melted chocolate, stir until well blended. Fold egg mixture into chocolate-cream mixture with creme de menthe.

Sift together flour, salt and bicarbonate of soda; add to creamed mixture. Pour into crumb crust in 8 in. springform pan.

Bake in slow oven 55 to 60 minutes. Allow to cool, then refrigerate.

Top with whipped cream.

Chocolate Ripple Cheesecake

Crumb Crust:

8 oz. plain sweet biscuits	4 oz. butter

Filling:

1 oz. dark chocolate	1 teaspoon grated lemon rind
1 lb. packaged cream cheese	2 tablespoons lemon juice
1¼ cups sugar	
6 eggs, separated	1 teaspoon vanilla
½ cup plain flour	1 cup cream

Crumb Crust: Crush biscuits. Combine biscuit crumbs and melted butter, press over base of 10 in. springform pan.

Refrigerate until set.

Filling: Melt chocolate in top of double saucepan over hot water. Beat together cheese and sugar until creamy. Beat in egg-yolks until just blended. Stir in sifted flour, lemon rind and juice and vanilla. Beat egg-whites until they form soft peaks. Beat cream until stiff. Fold beaten egg-whites, then whipped cream into cheese mixture, stir until thoroughly blended. Spoon 1/3 of mixture over prepared crumb crust; drizzle about 1 teaspoon of melted chocolate over; repeat twice, ending with chocolate. Cut through mixture with long thin knife to swirl chocolate, so forming marble effect. Stand pan on baking tray. Bake in slow oven 45 minutes. Turn off heat, leave in oven with door closed 1 hour longer. Leave until completely cold before cutting.

Chocolate Rum Cheesecake

Chocolate Crumb Crust:

8 oz. plain chocolate biscuits	¼ teaspoon cinnamon
4 oz. butter	¼ teaspoon nutmeg

Filling:

1 lb. cream cheese	½ teaspoon vanilla
3 eggs	2 oz. dark chocolate
½ cup castor sugar	1 tablespoon rum

Topping:

1 cup cream	1 tablespoon rum

Chocolate Crumb Crust: Crush biscuits finely, place in bowl. Add spices and mix. Melt butter and add to crumb mixture, pressing together to make a shortbread. Line base and sides of 8 in. springform pan with this mixture, pressing on firmly.

Refrigerate thoroughly.

Filling: Press cheese through fine strainer; beat eggs very well until thick. Add sugar. continue beating until lemon-coloured. Continue beating while adding cheese gradually. Beat until mixture is smooth. Divide mixture equally into 2. Add vanilla to one portion and spread into prepared crumb crust. Melt chocolate, beat into second portion, with rum. Spoon over vanilla mixture.

Bake in moderate oven 45 minutes or until set. Remove, cool.

Topping: Whip cream until stiff, add rum, stir in. Spread over surface of cold cheesecake.

Decorate with grated chocolate.

Ripple Cheesecake

Pastry:

¾ cup plain flour	1 egg-yolk
¾ cup self-raising flour	1 dessertspoon castor sugar
3 oz. butter	1 tablespoon water, approx.

Filling:

12 oz. cream cheese	2 oz. dark chocolate
2 egg-whites	**Topping:**
½ cup sugar	3 oz. dark chocolate
2 tablespoons cream	½ oz. solid white vegetable shortening
½ teaspoon vanilla	

Pastry: Rub butter into sifted flours until mixture resembles fine breadcrumbs; add sugar. Mix with yolk and sufficient water to give a firm dough. Roll out on lightly floured surface and line 8 in. fluted flan ring or sandwich tin.

Refrigerate 30 minutes.

Filling: Press cheese through sieve, mix in cream and beat until smooth; add vanilla. Beat egg-whites until soft, gradually beating in sugar to make meringue mixture. Fold meringue into cheese mixture until evenly mixed. Pour ⅓ of cheese mixture into prepared case, then drizzle 1 tablespoon of the melted chocolate over. Repeat until pastry case is filled, finishing with cheese mixture.

Bake in hot oven 10 minutes, then reduce heat to moderate and cook 25 to 30 minutes; cool.

Topping: Melt chopped chocolate and shortening over gentle heat, spread over cooled cheesecake.

Colonial Curd Cake

Pastry:

3 oz. butter	1 egg-yolk
¼ cup castor sugar	1¼ cups plain flour

Filling:

1 lb. cream cheese	2 tablespoons milk
2 oz. butter	3 large eggs, separated
½ teaspoon vanilla	1½ tablespoons cornflour
1 dessertspoon grated lemon rind	½ cup evaporated milk or cream
⅔ cup sugar	

Pastry: Cream butter and sugar. Mix in egg-yolk, then the sifted flour.

Roll out pastry and line 8 in. springform pan.

Filling: Sieve cream cheese. Cream softened butter with half the sugar, the vanilla, and grated lemon rind. Add remaining sugar and milk, mix well.

Beat in egg-yolks and cornflour, then sieved cheese in alternate quantities with evaporated milk or cream. Fold in softly beaten egg-whites.

Pour into prepared pastry.

Bake in hot oven 10 minutes, reduce heat to moderately slow, bake a further 40 to 50 minutes or until nearly set in centre. Turn off heat, leave cake in oven at least 15 minutes.

Cool, cover with whipped cream, sprinkle with nutmeg.

Refrigerate for several hours before serving.

Wonderful Basic Cheesecake—firm textured, deliciously rich—is one of the most popular of all cheesecakes. Topping is whipped cream sprinkled with cinnamon or nutmeg (see page 8).

Continental Cheesecake

1 lb. cream cheese
1 cup castor sugar
2 eggs
¼ pint sour cream
pinch nutmeg

1 tablespoon castor
  sugar, extra
3 oz. plain sweet biscuits

Crush biscuits and add pinch of nutmeg. Sprinkle on base of greased 7 in. sandwich tin with removable base. Sieve cream cheese, beat in sugar and eggs. Spoon on to biscuit mixture, bake in moderate oven 30 minutes.

Mix sour cream with extra sugar and spread over top of cheese mixture. Return to oven, bake further 12 to 15 minutes; leave to cool in oven with door ajar.

Refrigerate before serving.

Cream-Topped Cake

Cake Base:

1 cup self-raising flour
¼ teaspoon salt
4 oz. butter
½ teaspoon vanilla

⅔ cup castor sugar
2 eggs
1 dessertspoon milk

Filling:

8 oz. packaged cream
  cheese
⅔ cup sugar

½ cup sour cream
1 teaspoon vanilla
2 eggs

Topping:

1 cup sour cream
2 tablespoons sugar

1 teaspoon lemon juice
1 tablespoon milk

Base: Cream together butter and castor sugar and beat until fluffy. Add eggs, one at a time, beating well after each addition. Stir in milk and vanilla. Add sifted flour and salt; blend well.
Filling: Cream cheese and sugar together. Add sour cream and vanilla. Mix well, then add eggs, one at a time; beat well together. Set aside.
Topping: Blend together sour cream and sugar. Add lemon juice and milk; mix well.

Turn cake mixture into well-greased and lightly floured 9 in. or 10 in. springform pan. Spread over bottom of pan and slightly hollow out centre. Spoon cream cheese filling over base.

Bake in moderately slow oven 50 to 60 minutes. Remove from oven, carefully spread over topping.

Bake further 5 minutes. Remove from oven; cool.

Refrigerate several hours or until set.

Cottage Cheesecake

1½ lb. cottage cheese
1 tablespoon rum
4 egg-whites
1 cup sugar

¼ pint cream
2 oz. dark chocolate
8 in. crumb crust

Press cottage cheese through sieve, mix with rum until soft and creamy. Beat egg-whites until they form soft peaks, then gradually beat in sugar. Fold into cheese until well blended; spoon into crumb crust.

Bake in moderate oven 25 minutes.

Cool, then refrigerate. Whip cream, gradually beat in melted chocolate, spread over top.

Refrigerate again until topping has set.

Custard Cream Tart

Pastry:

½ cup self-raising
  flour
2½ tablespoons
  custard powder
1 cup plain flour

2½ tablespoons cornflour
1 dessertspoon icing
  sugar
4 oz. butter
water to mix

Filling:

4 oz. packaged
  cream cheese
½ cup sugar
3 eggs
¾ pint milk

½ teaspoon vanilla
¼ pint cream
1 tablespoon rum
¼ cup sultanas
nutmeg

Pastry: Sift dry ingredients into bowl. Rub in butter until mixture resembles breadcrumbs. Mix to a stiff dough with water (approximately 2 tablespoons).

Refrigerate 1 hour.

Roll out pastry on lightly floured board, line greased 9 in. pie-plate. Pinch edge decoratively. Brush base of empty pastry case with egg-white (use a little of white from one of the eggs in filling).

Refrigerate while preparing filling.
Filling: Beat well together the cheese and sugar. Add the eggs, beat until just blended. Warm milk, gradually beat into egg-and-cheese mixture. Add vanilla, cream, and rum. Sprinkle sultanas over base of pie shell.

Carefully spoon filling into pie case. Sprinkle top with a little nutmeg.

Bake in hot oven 10 minutes, reduce heat to moderate, cook further 40 to 45 minutes or until set.

Cool, then refrigerate.

Cream Cheese Cake

Base:

3 oz. butter
⅓ cup icing sugar
1 egg-yolk

1 cup self-raising flour
2 tablespoons milk or
 water

Topping:

8 oz. packaged
 cream cheese
2 egg-yolks
3 egg-whites
½ oz butter

¼ cup castor sugar
½ teaspoon vanilla
1 dessertspoon grated
 lemon rind

Base: Beat together butter and sifted sugar until light and fluffy. Add unbeaten egg-yolk, mix in lightly. Gradually stir in sifted flour. Add milk or water, mix well (mixture should be of fairly stiff consistency). Spread in greased 8 in. springform pan lined with band of greased greaseproof paper.

Bake in moderately hot oven 15 to 20 minutes, or until pale golden colour; cool.

Topping: Beat cream cheese until smooth. Stir in unbeaten egg-yolks, softened butter, and sugar. Blend well together, then add vanilla and lemon rind. Fold in softly beaten egg-whites. Spoon over cooled base.

Return to moderate oven, cook further 15 to 20 minutes,

Cool completely, carefully remove from tin.

Cream Cheese and Sultana Tart

Pastry:

1 cup plain flour
pinch salt

4 oz. butter
3 tablespoons cream

Filling:

½ lb. cottage cheese
4 oz. packaged
 cream cheese
1 tablespoon cornflour
2 tablespoons cream

3 eggs, separated
¾ cup sugar
1 teaspoon vanilla
3 tablespoons sultanas

Pastry: Sift flour and salt into bowl, rub in butter. Add cream, mix until a smooth ball is formed. Refrigerate 2 hours, then roll out and line deep 9 in. pie plate; decorate edges.

Filling: Sieve cheeses, beat until smooth. Add cornflour, cream, egg-yolks, and sugar, beat well. Add vanilla and sultanas, mix well. Beat egg-whites until soft peaks form. Fold into the cheese mixture carefully.

Pour into the prepared pie case.

Bake in moderate oven 50 minutes or until brown.

Fruit Cheesecake

Crumb Crust:

6 oz. plain sweet
 biscuits
2 tablespoons
 powdered milk

1 tablespoon water
3 oz. butter

Filling:

8 oz. packaged
 cream cheese
½ cup castor sugar
2 eggs

3 tablespoons powdered
 milk
1 teaspoon vanilla
15 oz. can fruit cocktail

Crumb Crust: Crush biscuits, add powdered milk. Melt butter, add to biscuit mixture with water. Press on to base and round sides of greased 7 in. sandwich tin with removable base.

Filling: Strain fruit well, divide in half. Cream together cheese and sugar, add powdered milk. Add eggs and vanilla, beat until smooth. Add half well-drained fruit. Pour into crumb crust.

Bake in moderate oven 30 to 40 minutes or until set.

Remove from oven, cool.

Topping: Whip ¼ pint cream until stiff, fold in remaining drained fruit, chopped, spread over surface of cheesecake.

Hazelnut Cheesecake

Crumb Crust:

5 oz. plain sweet
 biscuits

3 oz. butter
2 oz. ground hazelnuts

Filling:

12 oz. packaged cream
 cheese
½ cup sugar
2 eggs
chopped hazelnuts

1 dessertspoon custard
 powder
1 teaspoon vanilla
1 tablespoon lemon juice

Crumb Crust: Crush biscuits finely, melt butter. Combine all ingredients. Press on to base and up sides of 7 in. greased sandwich tin with removable base.

Refrigerate until firm.

Filling: Cream together cheese and sugar until light and fluffy. Add eggs, one at a time, beating well after each addition. Add custard powder, vanilla, and lemon juice; beat well.

Pour mixture into prepared crumb crust.

Bake in slow oven 40 minutes. Fifteen minutes before end of cooking time, sprinkle a few chopped hazelnuts over top. At end of cooking time, turn off heat, leave to cool in oven.

Refrigerate several hours or overnight.

Honey Cheesecake

Pastry:

1 cup plain flour	3 oz. butter
⅓ cup fine semolina	1 tablespoon castor sugar
pinch salt	water to mix

Filling:

3 tablespoons sultanas	1 tablespoon fine
1 tablespoon mixed	semolina
peel	3 tablespoons cream
12 oz. cottage cheese	1 tablespoon lemon juice
3 eggs, separated	1 tablespoon sugar
3 tablespoons honey	1 teaspoon cinnamon

Pastry: In bowl, sift together flour, semolina, and salt. Rub in butter, add sugar. Add sufficient cold water to mix to a stiff dough (approximately 2 teaspoons). Press pastry with floured fingers on to bottom and three-quarters of the way up sides of 8 in. springform pan.

Refrigerate.

Filling: Sprinkle chopped fruit over bottom of pastry case. Sieve cheese into large bowl. Add egg-yolks, honey, semolina, cream, and lemon juice to cheese; beat well. Lastly fold in softly beaten egg-whites. Pour cheese mixture over fruit, sprinkle top with combined sugar and cinnamon.

Bake in hot oven 10 minutes. Reduce heat to moderate, bake further 30 minutes or until set.

Hungarian Pineapple Cheesecake

Pastry:

2 oz. butter	1½ cups plain flour
2 egg-yolks	½ teaspoon baking-
1 tablespoon lemon	powder
juice	1 tablespoon cold water
pinch salt	

Filling:

6 oz. cream cheese	15 oz. can crushed
1 cup sour cream	pineapple
⅓ cup sugar	½ cup chopped raisins
pinch salt	whipped cream
3 eggs	
1 teaspoon grated	
lemon rind	

Pastry: Cream butter until light and fluffy, beat in egg-yolks, salt, and lemon juice. Combine with sifted dry ingredients, work to firm dough with water.

Refrigerate 1 hour. Roll out to ¼ in. thickness, press with fingers over base and sides of 8 in. springform pan.

Refrigerate further 1 hour.

Filling: Rub cream cheese through sieve, add sour cream, sugar, salt, well-beaten eggs, (reserve a little egg-white), and grated lemon rind; beat well together. Brush pastry case with reserved egg-white, sprinkle evenly with drained pineapple and raisins.

Carefully pour cheese mixture over.

Bake in hot oven 10 minutes, reduce heat to moderate, cook further 20 minutes or until nicely browned.

Cool, then refrigerate.

Decorate with whipped cream.

Italian Apple Cream Pie

Pastry:

1¼ cups plain flour	2 teaspoons grated
½ teaspoon salt	lemon rind
½ teaspoon cinnamon	4 oz. butter
¼ cup sugar	1 egg-yolk
1 teaspoon baking	2 tablespoons sherry
powder	

Filling:

2 apples	½ cup cream
2 eggs	8 oz. packaged cream
½ cup sugar	cheese
2 tablespoons plain	1 tablespoon mixed peel
flour	¼ cup raisins
2 teaspoons grated	¼ teaspoon salt
lemon rind	

Pastry: Sift together dry ingredients, add grated lemon rind. With pastry blender or 2 knives, cut in butter. Beat egg-yolk and sherry together. Add to flour mixture; mix well, forming smooth ball. Roll out, line square 8 in. slab tin; trim edges.

Filling: Peel and core apples, cut into quarters, then slice thinly. Arrange in overlapping lines in pastry shell.

Beat eggs and sugar until thick; gradually add sifted flour, lemon rind, cream, softened cream cheese, peel, chopped raisins, and salt. Pour over apple.

Bake in moderate oven 1 to 1¼ hours.

Serve slightly warm or cold with whipped cream.

Strawberry-glazed Cheesecake has a crumb crust at the base only. Topping is halved fresh strawberries, with a fresh-strawberry glaze spooned over (see page 18).

Baked Lemon Cheesecake

8 oz. packaged cream cheese	1 tablespoon grated lemon rind
8 oz. bulk cream cheese	⅓ cup lemon juice
⅔ cup castor sugar	2 tablespoons plain flour
2 eggs	8 in. crumb crust
½ cup sour cream	

Beat together sieved cheeses and sugar until smooth; beat in eggs 1 at a time, beating well after addition; beat in sour cream, flour, lemon rind each and juice. Pour into crumb crust, bake in moderately slow oven 1 to 1¼ hours, or until surface is firm to touch.

Lemon-Topped Cheesecake

1½ lb. cream cheese	1 cup sugar
1 tablespoon rum	9 in. crumb crust
4 egg-whites	

Topping:

⅔ cup sugar	1½ tablespoons lemon juice
1½ tablespoons cornflour	1 dessertspoon grated lemon rind
pinch salt	½ teaspoon vanilla
½ oz. butter	
¾ cup boiling water	
1 egg	

Press cream cheese through sieve, mix with rum until soft and smooth. Beat egg-whites until soft, gradually add sugar, continue beating until of meringue consistency. Fold meringue into cheese mixture until well blended.

Pour into prepared crust, bake in moderate oven 25 minutes.

Cool, spread over the Lemon Topping. Refrigerate.

Just before serving, pipe whipped cream decoratively round edge.

Topping: Mix together sugar, cornflour, rind, and salt. Slowly add to boiling water, cook over low heat, stirring until mixture boils and thickens. Add some of hot mixture to beaten egg, then stir back into remaining mixture, with the butter; cook 2 minutes more.

Remove from heat, blend in lemon juice and vanilla.

Cool before spreading over cheesecake.

Luscious Gourmet Cheesecake

1½ lb. cream cheese	1 whole egg, extra
1½ cups castor sugar	1½ cups sour cream
2½ dessertspoons plain flour	¼ cup lemon juice
pinch salt	3 tablespoons castor sugar, extra
6 eggs, separated	9 in. crumb crust

Filling: Beat sieved cream cheese until softened, combine with sugar, flour, and salt, beat well. Beat in the whole egg plus the 6 egg-yolks, sour cream, and lemon juice.

Beat egg-whites until stiff but not dry; beat in extra sugar, fold into cream cheese mixture.

Pour into prepared crumb crust, bake in slow oven 1¼ to 1½ hours. Allow to cool in oven. Refrigerate until nicely firm.

Papaw Cream Cheese Tart

Biscuit Pastry:

3 oz. butter	1⅔ cups plain flour
¼ cup sugar	½ teaspoon baking powder
1 egg	

Filling:

3 passionfruit	1 dessertspoon grated orange rind
2 cups chopped papaw	2 tablespoons sugar

Topping:

2 oz. butter	1 dessertspoon grated lemon rind
10 oz. cream cheese	1 tablespoon lemon juice
2 eggs	¼ cup sugar

Biscuit Pastry: Cream butter, sugar, and egg together, work in sifted flour and baking powder, turn on to floured board, knead lightly until smooth. Roll pastry, line 9 in. pie plate being careful not to break or stretch the pastry. Trim and decorate edge.

Spoon filling into pastry case, spread carefully with topping.

Bake in moderately hot oven for 10 minutes, redue heat to moderate, bake for further 15 to 20 minutes or until set.

Cool before serving.

Filling: Remove pulp from passionfruit, combine with papaw, orange rind, and sugar.

Topping: Sieve cream cheese. Cream butter, cream cheese, lemon rind and juice until smooth. Beat eggs until foamy, gradually add sugar and continue beating until sugar is dissolved, fold into cream-cheese mixture.

Passionfruit Cheesecake

1 lb. packaged cream cheese	1 tablespoon lemon juice
½ cup sugar	1 teaspoon vanilla
3 eggs, separated	½ cup cream
¼ cup plain flour	pulp of 3 passionfruit
1 teaspoon grated lemon rind	8 in. crumb crust

Soften cream cheese, gradually beat in sugar until light and fluffy.

Beat in egg-yolks until just blended, stir in sifted flour, lemon rind, juice, and vanilla. Beat egg-whites until they form soft peaks. Beat cream until stiff.

Fold beaten egg-whites, then cream into egg-yolk mixture with 1 tablespoon of passionfruit. Spoon into prepared crumb case; bake in slow oven 40 minutes to 1 hour; turn off heat. Leave in oven 1 hour longer.

Cool, then refrigerate.

Top with remaining passionfruit.

Delicious Cheesecake

Crumb Crust:

6 oz. plain sweet biscuits	3 oz. butter

Filling:

1 lb. packaged cream cheese	½ cup plain flour
1 cup sugar	2 teaspoons grated lemon rind
3 eggs	1 tablespoon lemon juice
¼ teaspoon salt	1 cup sour cream

Crumb Crust: Crush biscuits. Combine crumbs and melted butter. Press mixture on to base of 9 in. greased springform pan.

Refrigerate until firm.

Filling: Beat cream cheese until smooth, add sugar; beat well. Add eggs, 1 at a time, beating well after each addition, Add salt, lemon rind, lemon juice, sifted flour, and sour cream; beat well. Pour cheese mixture on to crumb crust.

Bake in moderately slow oven ¾ hour. Turn off oven heat.

Cool in oven 30 minutes.

Refrigerate.

Spread top with whipped cream before serving, sprinkle with nutmeg or cinnamon.

Note: This is a beautifully textured cheesecake. Toward the end of cooking time, or while it cools, it may crack a little across the top. This is a characteristic of many cheesecakes.

Pineapple-Wine Tart

½ lb. cream cheese	1 teaspoon vanilla
1 cup sugar	15 oz. can crushed pineapple
2 oz. butter	1 tablespoon cornflour
½ cup plain flour	½ cup sweet white wine
½ teaspoon salt	9 in. unbaked pastry case
2 eggs	
¾ cup milk	

Rub cream cheese through fine sieve, gradually beat in sugar. Add softened butter, beat until light. Sift flour with salt, blend in. Add eggs one at a time, alternately with milk; beat in vanilla.

Drain pineapple, retaining about 3 tablespoons of syrup with the fruit. Place over gentle heat; when hot, stir in the cornflour blended with wine. Cook 1 minute, stirring; cool, spread over base of pastry case. Pour over cheese mixture.

Bake in hot oven 10 minutes, reduce temperature to moderate, bake further 30 minutes or until filling is set. Cool, then refrigerate.

Pineapple Cream Cheese Tart

Shortcrust Pastry:

1½ cups plain flour	pinch salt
½ teaspoon baking powder	4 oz. butter
	1 dessertspoon water, approx.

Filling:

15 oz. can crushed pineapple	½ cup sugar, extra
⅓ cup sugar	2 eggs
1 tablespoon cornflour	½ cup milk
8 oz. cream cheese	½ teaspoon vanilla

Shortcrust Pastry: Rub butter into sifted dry ingredients until mixture resembles fine breadcrumbs. Add sufficient water to combine ingredients. Turn pastry on to floured board, roll to fit an 8 in. pie plate. Trim and decorate edge.

Refrigerate while preparing filling.

Filling: Combine undrained pineapple, ⅓ cup sugar, and cornflour in saucepan, stir until mixture boils and thickens. When cold, spread into uncooked pastry case. Sieve cream cheese, beat until smooth, add extra sugar, eggs, milk, and vanilla, beat well to combine; pour over pineapple mixture.

Bake in moderately hot oven 10 minutes, reduce heat to moderate for further 25 to 30 minutes. Cool, then refrigerate.

Sherried Cheesecake

1 lb. packaged cream cheese	¼ cup sweet sherry
3 eggs	1 teaspoon lemon juice
	8 in. crumb crust

Beat together cheese and sugar until smooth and fluffy. Add eggs one at a time, beating well after each addition.

Add lemon juice and sherry; beat well. Pour into crumb crust. Bake in slow oven 40 to 45 minutes or until mixture is firm. Allow to cool in oven, Refrigerate.

Top with whipped cream before serving.

Strawberry-glazed Cheesecake

Crumb Crust:

6 oz. plain sweet biscuits	3 oz. butter

Filling:

1½ lb. cream cheese	¼ pint sour cream
¼ cup self-raising flour	2 eggs
1 dessertspoon grated lemon rind	¾ cup sugar
	¾ cup milk

Strawberry Glaze:

1 punnet strawberries	3 dessertspoons cornflour
½ cup water	¼ cup sugar

Crumb Crust: Crush biscuits finely, add melted butter and combine well. Press over base only of 8 in. springform pan.
Filling: Beat together sieved cream cheese, sifted flour, grated rind, and sour cream. Beat eggs and sugar together until light and fluffy, add milk. Gradually beat in cheese mixture. Pour mixture on to crumb crust. Bake in a moderately slow oven 1½ hours.
Strawberry Glaze: Crush ½ of the strawberries, add the water and cook 2 minutes; strain. Mix cornflour with sugar, stir into strained strawberry liquid. Stir until mixture boils and thickens. (A few drops of red colouring can be added.) Cool slightly. Cut remaining strawberries in ½ and arrange on top of cooled cheesecake; spoon glaze over. Refrigerate.

Strawberry-Topped Cheesecake

Crumb Crust:

4 oz. coconut biscuits	2 oz. butter

Filling:

8 oz. packaged cream cheese	1 teaspoon vanilla pinch salt
½ cup sugar	½ pint cream
3 egg-yolks	2 egg-whites
1½ tablespoons plain flour	

Topping:

fresh strawberries	1½ tablespoons sweet sherry
½ cup red currant jelly	

Crumb Crust: Crush biscuits and combine with melted butter. Press mixture on to base of greased 8 in. springform pan. Refrigerate until firm.
Filling: In bowl, beat together cheese and sugar until smooth and fluffy. Add egg-yolks, beat well. Add sifted flour, vanilla and salt, beating continually. Gradually pour in hot scalded cream, beating all the time. Lastly fold in softly beaten egg-whites. Pour cheese mixture on to crumb crust.

Stand pan on oven tray, bake in slow oven 1½ hours. Cool, then refrigerate.
Topping: Place jelly and sherry in a saucepan. Dissolve over low heat, stirring with a wooden spoon. Refrigerate until commencing to set. Decorate cake when cold with strawberries cut into quarters. Spoon jelly mixture over, refrigerate until set.

Sultana Cream Cheesecake

12 oz. packaged cream cheese	2 tablespoons sultanas
1 egg	1 oz. slivered almonds
½ cup sugar	7 in. crumb crust
1 dessertspoon grated lemon rind	

Beat cream cheese until soft. Beat in egg, sugar, and lemon rind; beat until light and fluffy. Stir in sultanas. Spoon into crumb crust, sprinkle with almonds.

Bake in slow oven 30 to 35 minutes. Cool, then refrigerate.

Just before serving, decorate with whipped cream.

Superb Sour Cream Cheesecake combines cottage cheese, cream cheese and sour cream in the velvety-textured filling (see page 20).

Sultana Cheesecake

Pastry:

1 cup plain flour	1 tablespoon icing
½ cup self-raising	sugar
flour	4 oz. butter
2 tablespoons custard	2 tablespoons water,
powder	approx.
2 tablespoons	
cornflour	

Filling:

8 oz. cottage cheese	1 tablespoon milk
1 oz. butter	1 dessertspoon grated
¼ cup sugar	lemon rind
1 egg	¼ cup sultanas

Pastry: Sift dry ingredients into basin, rub in butter until mixture resembles fine breadcrumbs. Mix to a stiff dough with water; refrigerate 1 hour.

Roll out ⅔ of the dough on floured board, line the base and up the sides of 7 in. greased sandwich tin with removable base.

Filling: Rub cheese through sieve. Cream butter until light and fluffy, beat in sugar. Add egg, beat well. Add cheese, milk, lemon rind, and sultanas. Spread in pastry case. Roll out remaining ⅓ of pastry. Place pastry in position on top of cheesecake, trim edges. Slash pastry top neatly in 2 or 3 places.

Bake in hot oven 15 minutes. Reduce heat and bake further 25 to 30 minutes in moderately hot oven until pastry is light golden and crisp.

Leave in tin until cold; refrigerate overnight.

Sprinkle with icing sugar before serving.

Superb Sour Cream Cheesecake

8 oz. packaged cream	1 cup sour cream
cheese	1 dessertspoon grated
8 oz. cottage cheese	lemon rind
3 eggs	3 tablespoons lemon
1 cup sugar	juice
2 tablespoons cornflour	8 in. crumb crust

Sieve cheeses, beat together until smooth. Add eggs, one at a time, beating well after each addition. Add cornflour and sugar, mix well. Blend in sour cream, lemon rind, and juice. Pour mixture into crumb crust. Stand pan on oven tray.

Bake in moderately slow oven 50 to 60 minutes; cool in oven. Refrigerate several hours before serving.

Dark Chocolate Cheesecake

Crumb Crust:

5 oz. plain chocolate	2 oz. butter
biscuits	¼ teaspoon cinnamon

Filling:

5 oz. dark chocolate	2 eggs
1 lb. packaged cream	1 dessertspoon cocoa
cheese	1 teaspoon vanilla
¾ cup sugar	1 cup sour cream

Crumb Crust: Crush biscuits. Combine crushed biscuits, cinnamon, and melted butter in bowl. Press mixture on to base of greased 8 in. spring-form pan. Refrigerate until set.

Note: If using plain sweet biscuits in place of chocolate biscuits, omit ½ oz. butter, add 1 oz. melted dark chocolate.

Filling: Melt chopped chocolate in top of double saucepan. Cream together cheese and sugar until smooth and fluffy. Add eggs, one at a time, beating well after each addition. Add cocoa, chocolate, vanilla, and sour cream; beat well. Pour cheese mixture on to crumb crust.

Stand pan on oven tray, bake in slow oven 1 hour 10 minutes. The cake might still be moist in centre, but will set as it cools. Turn off oven heat. Cool in oven with door slightly ajar, then refrigerate.

Decorate with whipped cream and grated chocolate.

Cheesecake Slices

Recipes for baked and unbaked slices are given in this section. Cut them into squares or slices. Delicious for special luncheons, afternoon tea, dessert

Apple Cheese Slice

Pastry:

1½ cups plain flour
½ teaspoon baking powder
½ teaspoon cinnamon
¼ teaspoon ground ginger
¼ teaspoon salt
¼ teaspoon ground cloves
¼ cup brown sugar
4 oz. butter
1 tablespoon sherry
approx. 2 tablespoons milk

Filling:

2 large apples
8 oz. packaged cream cheese
½ cup sugar
14 oz. can sweetened condensed milk
½ teaspoon salt
½ cup lemon juice
1 dessertspoon grated lemon rind
3 eggs
½ teaspoon vanilla
⅓ cup coconut
½ cup sultanas
1 tablespoon plain flour

Pastry: Sift dry ingredients into bowl. Cut in butter with knife.

Add milk and sherry, lightly blend until of dough consistency.

Roll out dough on floured board to line base of greased 7 in. x 11 in. lamington tin.

Refrigerate while preparing filling.

Filling: Peel and core apples, cut into quarters, then slice thinly; arrange in overlapping lines on refrigerated pastry base.

Beat together cream cheese and sugar until smooth. Add eggs, one at a time, beating well after each addition.

Add condensed milk, salt, lemon juice and rind, vanilla, coconut, and sifted flour, beating continuously; fold in sultanas. Pour cheese mixture over apples.

Bake in moderate oven 20 minutes.

Reduce heat to moderately slow, bake further 40 minutes or until cooked.

Cool, then refrigerate. Cut into slices.

Apricot Slice

Pastry:

2 cups plain flour
4 oz. butter
2 tablespoons sugar
1 egg
3 tablespoons milk

Filling:

4 oz. dried apricots
1 tablespoon sugar
10 oz. cream cheese
2 oz. butter
¼ cup sugar, extra
2 eggs, separated
1 tablespoon milk
1 dessertspoon grated lemon rind

Pastry: Sift flour, rub in butter, add sugar. Add milk, lightly beaten egg, mix lightly. Turn on to floured board, knead gently; refrigerate 30 minutes. Divide in 2 portions (approx. ⅔ and ⅓). Roll out larger portion, fit in greased 7 in. x 11 in. lamington tin, bringing pastry a little up sides; prick lightly.

Bake in moderate oven 10 minutes, remove and cool.

Filling: Soak apricots in little water to cover ½ hour, then simmer gently until tender, adding sugar toward end of cooking.

Cool, drain well. Spread over base.

Press cream cheese through sieve. Cream butter and extra sugar; beat in egg-yolks; add the cream cheese, milk and lemon rind.

Beat egg-whites until soft, then fold into cheese mixture. Spread over apricot mixture. Roll out remaining pastry, cut into ½ in. strips. Place lattice fashion on top of filling.

Glaze pastry with a little milk or egg-yolk.

Bake in moderate oven further 25 to 30 minutes.

Cool, cut into squares.

Banana Cream Cheese Slice

Pastry:

1½ cups plain flour	3 oz. butter
pinch salt	1 small egg
3 tablespoons sugar	

Filling:

2 oz. butter	3 bananas
¼ cup sugar	1 dessertspoon grated
2 eggs	lemon rind
6 oz. packaged	¼ cup lemon juice
cream cheese	2 oz. raisins

Pastry: Sift flour, salt, and sugar in basin, rub in the butter. Mix to a firm dough with beaten egg. Knead on lightly floured surface, divide into ⅓ and ⅔ portions.

Roll out large portion and line greased 7 in. x 11 in. lamington tin.

Prick base and sides, bake in moderate oven 10 minutes.

Remove from oven and cool.

Filling: Separate eggs, mash bananas; cream butter and sugar, beat in egg-yolks. Beat in softened cream cheese, banana, rind and juice of lemon, and chopped raisins. Beat egg-whites softly, fold into mixture. Spread over cold partly-cooked pastry.

Roll out remaining portion of pastry, cut into ½ in. strips, place crisscross or lattice fashion on top of filling.

Return to moderate oven and bake further 20 to 25 minutes.

Cool in tin, then cut into slices.

Chocolate Swirl Slice

Crumb Crust:

5 oz. plain sweet	1 tablespoon drinking
biscuits	chocolate
	3 oz. butter

Filling:

½ cup water	8 oz. packaged cream
3 teaspoons gelatine	cheese
1 cup sugar	14½ oz. can evaporated
1½ teaspoons vanilla	milk
	¼ cup cocoa

Crumb Crust: Crush biscuits, add drinking chocolate and melted butter; mix well.

Press crumb mixture on to the base of a 7 in. x 11 in. lamington tin; refrigerate.

Filling: Soften gelatine in water, dissolve over hot water; stir in ½ cup sugar and ½ cup evaporated milk; cool. Put remaining evaporated milk into cake pan, freeze until icicles form..

Beat together cream cheese and the remaining sugar, add vanilla. Blend in the gelatine mixture.

Whip frozen milk until it forms stiff peaks.

Fold into the cream cheese mixture. Place ⅓ of mixture into small bowl. Blend a little of mixture with the sifted cocoa, fold blended cocoa into the ⅓ portion.

Alternately spoon vanilla and chocolate mixtures onto the crumb base. Smooth top gently. Take skewer and pull it through mixture at intervals to swirl.

Refrigerate overnight.

Cut into bars or squares.

Mocha Swirl Slice: When blending in cocoa for filling, blend in also 1 dessertspoon instant coffee powder.

Cheesecake Squares

1 cup plain flour	⅓ cup water
1 cup self-raising flour	1 teaspoon lemon juice
½ cup cornflour	½ cup apricot jam
¼ cup custard powder	egg yolk for
¼ cup icing sugar	glazing
6 oz. butter	

Filling:

3 oz. butter	½ teaspoon grated
2 eggs	lemon rind
¼ cup sugar	10 oz. cottage cheese
⅓ cup chopped raisins	¼ cup sour cream

Sift dry ingredients into basin, rub in butter until mixture resembles fine breadcrumbs. Mix to dry dough with water and lemon juice. Turn out on to floured board and knead lightly.

Divide in half, roll out one half to fit base of greased lamington tin, spread with apricot jam, then spread cheese filling over evenly.

Filling: Separate eggs. Cream butter, add egg-yolks, sugar, raisins, lemon rind, sieved cheese, and sour cream; mix well. Fold in softly beaten egg-whites, spread over pastry. Roll out remaining pastry, place on top of cream mixture. Trim edges, brush with beaten egg-yolk.

Bake in moderate oven 30 to 40 minutes; cool.

Cut into squares to serve.

Sprinkle with sifted icing sugar.

Cheesecake Squares—cheesecake in the continental style, with rich biscuit pastry, lightly lemon-flavoured filling with raisins. (See page 22).

Continental Cream Cheese Slice

Pastry:

1½ cups plain flour	½ teaspoon baking
½ cup custard powder	powder
2 tablespoons icing	4 oz. butter
sugar	milk

Filling:

10 oz. packaged	2 oz. sultanas
cream cheese	1 dessertspoon grated
2 oz. butter	lemon rind
2 eggs	1 tablespoon lemon
¼ cup sugar	juice

Pastry: Sift into basin the flour, custard powder, icing sugar, and baking powder. Rub in the butter, add sufficient milk to make into a stiff dough (approximately 2 to 3 tablespoons of milk).

Roll out ⅔ of the pastry and line 7 in. x 11 in. greased lamington tin, bringing pastry ½ in. up the sides.

Prick base and bake in moderate oven 10 minutes; cool.

Filling: Beat butter with cream cheese until soft and creamy. Beat eggs and sugar until light and fluffy. Gradually add to cream cheese mixture, beat until smooth. Fold in sultanas, lemon rind, and juice.

Smooth filling over cooled pastry shell. Cut remaining pastry into long strips and place diagonally over filling in lattice form.

Bake in moderate oven 35 to 45 minutes; while still warm, cut into slices; leave in tin until cool.

Refrigerate.

Custard Cream Slice

Crumb Crust:

6 oz. plain sweet biscuits 3 oz. butter

Filling:

1 lb. packaged	¼ cup chopped raisins
cream cheese	½ teaspoon vanilla
½ cup sugar	pinch salt
2 tablespoons plain	1 dessertspoon grated
flour	lemon rind
2 tablespoons sour	2 eggs
cream	

Crumb Crust: Crush biscuits, add melted butter, mix well. Press half crumb mixture on to base of greased, 8 in. square slab tin lined with greased greaseproof paper.

Reserve remainder.

Filling: Beat together softened cream cheese, sugar, sifted flour, sour cream, vanilla, salt, and grated lemon rind. Beat eggs until frothy, then lightly fold into cheese mixture. Stir in raisins.

Filling: Beat together cream cheese, sugar, flour, sour cream, vanilla, salt, and grated lemon rind. Beat eggs until frothy, then lightly fold into cheese mixture. Stir in raisins.

Pour on to crumb base, sprinkle with reserved crumb mixture.

Firm crumbs by lightly smoothing over with back of tablespoon.

Bake in moderate oven 50 to 60 minutes; cool.

Refrigerate overnight. Before serving, cut into squares or fingers.

Custard Cheese Slice

Pastry:

2 cups plain flour
½ teaspoon baking
powder
5 oz. butter
pinch salt
1 egg-yolk
1 tablespoon
lemon juice

Filling:

1 pint milk
¼ pt. cream
4 eggs
8 oz. packaged cream
cheese
1 tablespoon lemon juice
2 teaspoons vanilla
3 tablespoons sugar
cinnamon or nutmeg

Pastry: Sift dry ingredients, rub in butter until mixture resembles dry breadcrumbs. Mix into a dry dough with egg-yolk and lemon juice; add a teaspoon or two of water, if necessary. Turn on to lightly floured surface, knead into a smooth round.

Roll out, line 7 in. x 11 in. lamington tin, bringing pastry up sides of tin. Glaze with a little egg-white (taken from eggs for filling).

Bake 5 minutes in hot oven to seal surface of pastry. Remove from oven.

Filling: Warm milk. Beat eggs lightly, gradually pour in half the warmed milk. Beat cream cheese until smooth with sugar and vanilla. Add remaining half of milk. Combine both mixtures, stir in cream and lemon juice. Pour mixture into pastry case; sprinkle with cinnamon or nutmeg.

Bake in hot oven 10 minutes, reduce heat to slow, bake further 35 minutes or until set.

Remove from oven, cool, then refrigerate.

Cut into squares or slices.

Golden Cheesecake Squares

Pastry:

2 cups self-raising flour	4 oz. butter
pinch salt	2 eggs
1 teaspoon grated	½ cup sugar
lemon rind	¾ cup milk

Topping:

2 eggs, separated	1 dessertspoon grated
½ cup sugar	lemon rind
¾ cup raisins	1 tablespoon honey
¾ lb. cottage cheese	½ cup chopped almonds

Pastry: Sift flour and salt into basin, add grated lemon rind. Make a well in centre and mix in melted butter, sugar, slightly beaten eggs, and milk.

Blend well together.

Spread over base of greased and lined 7 in. x 11 in. lamington tin.

Topping: Combine egg-yolks with sugar and beat until thick and creamy, add chopped raisins, sieved cheese and grated lemon rind. Mix well, fold in softly beaten egg-whites. Spread over top of cake batter.

Drizzle over with honey and sprinkle with almonds.

Bake in moderate oven 30 minutes. Reduce heat to moderately slow and cook further 10 minutes or until topping is set and lightly browned. Remove from oven.

Cool slightly, cut into squares to serve.

Lemon Cream Cheese Slice

Crumb Base:

5 oz. plain sweet biscuits	2½ oz. butter
1 teaspoon cinnamon	

Filling:

8 oz. packaged	¼ cup sugar
cream cheese	1 tablespoon currants
1 teaspoon grated	1 dessertspoon
lemon rind	mixed peel
1 tablespoon lemon	2 eggs, separated
juice	

Crumb Base: Crush biscuits, add cinnamon, mix in melted butter. Press on to base of greased and lined 7 in. x 11 in. lamington tin.

Refrigerate.

Filling: Beat cream cheese and egg-yolks together, add grated lemon rind, juice, sugar, currants, and chopped peel. Beat egg-whites until soft peaks form, fold into cheese mixture. Spoon on to crumb base.

Bake in moderate oven 30 to 35 minutes; cool. Before serving, cut into slices.

Orange Cheese Slice

Crumb Crust:

6 oz. plain sweet biscuits	3 oz. butter

Filling:

1 tablespoon gelatine	2 egg-whites
¼ cup cold water	½ cup orange juice
¼ cup boiling water	1 tablespoon grated
10 oz. packaged	orange rind
cream cheese	1 tablespoon grated
¼ cup sugar	lemon rind

Orange Glaze:

1 dessertspoon gelatine	½ cup sugar
¼ cup cold water	1 cup orange juice

Crumb Crust: Crush biscuits. Combine crushed biscuits and melted butter.

Press mixture on to base of 7 in. x 11 in. lamington tin lined with aluminium foil.

Refrigerate.

Filling: Soften gelatine in cold water. Add boiling water, stir until gelatine is dissolved; cool.

Beat cream cheese until smooth, gradually add sugar, orange juice, and rinds. Add dissolved gelatine, beat thoroughly.

Fold in softly beaten egg-whites. Pour cheese mixture on to prepared crumb crust.

Refrigerate until firm.

Orange Glaze: Soften gelatine in cold water. Place sugar and strained orange juice in saucepan, stir until sugar dissolves.

Bring to boil, add softened gelatine, stir until glaze is clear. Remove from heat, allow to cool.

Cover top of cheese slice with glaze. Refrigerate; when firm, cut into slices.

Passionfruit Cheese Slice

Crumb Crust:

6 oz. coconut biscuits   3 oz. butter

Topping:

8 oz. cottage cheese   ¼ cup water
8 oz. cream cheese   ¼ cup lemon juice
14 oz. can sweetened   1 teaspoon grated lemon
  condensed milk   rind
4 passionfruit   2 teaspoons vinegar
1 dessertspoon gelatine   ¾ cup cream

Crumb Crust: Crush biscuits. Combine crumbs with melted butter. Press mixture on to base of 7 in. x 11 in. lamington tin, lined with aluminium foil.

Refrigerate until firm.

Topping: Soften gelatine in water, dissolve over hot water. Sieve cheeses. Beat together cheeses until smooth. Add condensed milk, lemon juice, dissolved gelatine, lemon rind, and vinegar.

Beat until mixture is creamy, fold in whipped cream. Carefully fold in pulp from 2 passionfruit. Pour mixture carefully on to crumb crust, spread smoothly. Spread remaining passionfruit on top.

Refrigerate until set.

Cut into slices.

Pineapple Cheese Slice

Crumb Crust:

6 oz. plain sweet biscuits 3 oz. butter

Topping:

½ cup drained, canned   1¼ cups boiling water
  crushed pineapple   1 teaspoon grated lemon
½ cup pineapple syrup   rind
  from can   ½ teaspoon vanilla
1 packet lemon jelly   ½ pint cream
8 oz. packaged
  cream cheese

Crumb Crust: Line 7 in. x 11 in. lamington tin with aluminium foil, bringing foil up and over sides. This enables slice to be removed easily from tin after it has set.

Crush biscuits, combine with melted butter; mix well. Press evenly across foil at base of tin.

Refrigerate until firm.

Topping: Dissolve jelly in boiling water; add pineapple syrup; cool. Beat together cream cheese, lemon rind, and vanilla until smooth.

Combine ½ cup jelly with drained pineapple.

Blend remaining jelly into cheese mixture, fold in the whipped cream, pour cheese mixture on to crumb crust.

Refrigerate until set, then spoon pineapple mixture on top, refrigerate until firm.

Cut into slices to serve.

Strawberry Cheese Slice

Crumb Crust:

8 oz. plain sweet   ½ teaspoon nutmeg or
  biscuits   cinnamon
4 oz. butter

Filling:

strawberry jam   ¼ teaspoon salt
½ cup brown sugar   1 dessertspoon grated
1 tablespoon plain flour   lemon rind
¼ teaspoon nutmeg or   1 tablespoon lemon juice
  cinnamon   3 eggs, separated
12 oz. packaged   1 cup sour cream
  cream cheese   ⅓ cup sugar

Crumb Crust: Crush biscuits, add nutmeg, stir in melted butter. Press on to base of greased and lined 7 in. x 11 in. lamington tin.

Spread jam lightly over crumb crust.

Filling: Blend brown sugar, sifted flour, nutmeg or cinnamon, salt, and softened cream cheese. Add grated lemon rind and juice. Beat in egg-yolks and sour cream; beat until smooth.

Beat egg-whites until soft peaks form, gradually beat in sugar; fold into cheese mixture. Spoon over crumb crust, smooth surface.

Bake in moderate oven 30 minutes, reduce heat to moderately slow, bake further 30 minutes.

Turn oven off, leave slice in oven until cool.

Dust top with icing sugar; cut into slices.

Black Currant Cheese Slice: Black currant jam can be substituted for strawberry jam in the above recipe, and is a delicious flavour contrast with the cream cheese topping.

At back, Chocolate Swirl Slice (see page 22), with Passionfruit Cheese Slice in front (see page 26). Delicious to serve as dessert, or for afternoon tea.

Sour Cream Slice

Pastry:

2½ cups plain flour	1 egg
8 oz. butter	1 dessertspoon rum
¼ cup sugar	1 tablespoon sour cream

Filling:

3 oz. butter	1 dessertspoon grated
2 eggs	lemon rind
¼ cup sugar	10 oz. packaged cream
½ teaspoon vanilla	cheese
⅓ cup raisins	¼ cup sour cream

Pastry: Sift flour, rub in butter. Add sugar, then egg, rum, and sour cream together. Mix to a fairly soft dough.

Refrigerate 1 hour.

Press half pastry on to base of greased 7 in. x 11 in. lamington tin.

Bake in moderate oven 10 minutes.

Refrigerate remaining half of pastry.

Filling: Separate eggs; cream butter, egg-yolks, vanilla, sugar, lemon rind, softened cheese, and sour cream. Fold in chopped raisins, then softly beaten egg-whites. Pour on to slightly cooled pastry.

Roll out remaining refrigerated pastry, place on filling. Brush with sugar glaze, made by dissolving 1 tablespoon sugar in 2 tablespoons hot water, allow to cool. Sprinkle with extra sugar.

Bake in moderate oven 35 to 40 minutes.

Cool, cut into slices.

Yoghurt and Honey Squares

Crumb Crust:

5 oz. plain sweet biscuits	1 dessertspoon honey
2½ oz. butter	

Filling:

1 cup yoghurt	1 teaspoon grated lemon
8 oz. packaged cream	rind
cheese	2 teaspoons gelatine
2 tablespoons honey	1 tablespoon water
½ teaspoon vanilla	

Crumb Crust: Crush biscuits. Melt butter and honey, add to biscuit crumbs; mix well. Press crumb mixture on to base of greased and lined 7 in. x 11 in. lamington tin.

Refrigerate.

Filling: Beat yoghurt, cream cheese, honey, vanilla, and lemon rind until smooth and creamy.

Fold in gelatine which has been softened in the water and dissolved over hot water. Pour on to base.

Refrigerate until firm.

Serve, cut into squares.

Pineapple Slice

Crumb Crust:

6 oz. plain sweet biscuits	3 oz. butter

Topping:

8 oz. packaged	15 oz. can crushed
cream cheese	pineapple
14 oz. can condensed	1 dessertspoon
milk	gelatine
	⅓ cup lemon juice

Crumb Crust: Crush biscuits, combine biscuit crumbs and melted butter, blend well. Press over base of 7 in. x 11 in. lamington tin, refrigerate until set.

Topping: Cream together cheese and condensed milk until light and smooth. Drain pineapple, reserving syrup. Sprinkle gelatine into pineapple syrup, stir over low heat until dissolved; cool. Add pineapple syrup and lemon juice to cheese mixture, beat well. Stir in drained pineapple. Pour on to prepared crumb crust.

Refrigerate until set.

Grapefruit Slice

Crumb Crust:

6 oz. plain sweet biscuits	3 oz. butter

Topping:

8 oz. packaged	2 grapefruit
cream cheese	14 oz. can
1 teaspoon grated	condensed milk
grapefruit rind	¼ cup lemon juice

Crumb Crust: Crush biscuits, combine with melted butter. Press over base of 7 in. x 11 in. lamington tin.

Refrigerate until set.

Topping: Remove all skin and pith from grapefruit. Cut grapefruit into segments over bowl so no juice is lost. Cut segments into small pieces. Beat cheese and grapefruit rind until creamy. Gradually beat in condensed milk and lemon juice, and any juice from grapefruit. Fold in chopped grapefruit. Pour on to prepared crumb crust.

Refrigerate until set.

Unbaked Cheesecakes

Unbaked cheesecakes—many of them with fresh fruit flavours—are a perfect light, lovely dessert

Apricot Cheese Tart

Crumb Crust:

6 oz. plain sweet biscuits

3 oz. butter
½ teaspoon nutmeg

Filling:

8 oz. cream cheese
½ cup sweetened condensed milk

2 tablespoons lemon juice
¼ pint cream

Topping:

1 cup apricot jam
2 tablespoons sugar

2 tablespoons water
1 teaspoon gelatine

Crumb Crust: Crush biscuits into fine crumbs, place in bowl with nutmeg. Melt butter, add to crumbs. Press firmly round sides and base of 9 in. pie plate.

Refrigerate while preparing filling.

Filling: Sieve cream cheese, add condensed milk and lemon juice; beat until smooth. Fold in whipped cream. Pour into prepared crumb crust.

Refrigerate while preparing topping.

Topping: Soften gelatine in 1 tablespoonful of the water. Combine jam, sugar and remaining water. Stir over heat until sugar dissolves, bring to boil. Boil, without stirring, 2 minutes. Remove from heat, strain; add softened gelatine, stir until dissolved. Cool slightly, spoon over cream cheese filling. Refrigerate well before serving.

Apricot Nectar Cheesecake

Base:

5 oz. plain sweet biscuits

2½ oz. butter

Filling:

15 oz. can apricot nectar
1 tablespoon gelatine
12 oz. packaged cream cheese

½ cup castor sugar
1 tablespoon lemon juice
½ pint cream

Topping:

1 tablespoon sugar
1½ dessertspoons arrowroot

1 dessertspoon rum

Base: Combine finely-crushed biscuits crumbs and melted butter; mix well. Press mixture firmly on to base of 8 in. springform pan; refrigerate 1 hour.

Filling: Measure 1 cup apricot nectar from can (reserve remainder for topping). Pour nectar into small saucepan, sprinkle gelatine over. Place over low heat and stir until gelatine is dissolved, allow to cool and thicken slightly.

Beat softened cream cheese and sugar until mixture is smooth and creamy, add lemon juice. Beat in apricot mixture, then fold in whipped cream. Pour mixture on to crumb base, refrigerate 2 hours or until firm.

Topping: Place sugar and arrowroot in saucepan, gradually stir in reserved apricot nectar. Bring mixture to the boil, stirring constantly, remove from heat, add rum. Continue stirring for a few minutes to allow mixture to cool slightly. Spread topping over cheese cake, return to refrigerator for 1 hour.

Note: Before loosening sides of springform pan, run a sharp knife around the edge of the cheesecake.

Snow-White Cheesecake

Base:

4 oz. plain sweet
  biscuits
1 teaspoon ground
  ginger
2 oz. butter

Topping:

8 oz. cottage cheese
8 oz. packaged cream
  cheese
½ cup castor sugar
1 teaspoon vanilla

1 dessertspoon
  gelatine
⅓ cup water
½ pint cream
2 egg-whites

Base: Crush biscuits finely, add ginger and melted butter. Press evenly over base of greased 8 in. springform pan. Refrigerate while preparing topping.

Topping: Sieve cottage cheese. Beat softened cream cheese until smooth and light; add cottage cheese, sugar and vanilla, beat well. Add gelatine to water, dissolve over hot water; cool. Gradually add cream to cheese mixture, beating constantly; add gelatine mixture, beat well. Beat egg-whites until soft peaks form, fold into cheese mixture. Spread evenly over base, refrigerate until firm.

Brandied Cheesecake

Sponge Layer:

1 egg, separated
2 tablespoons castor
  sugar
3½ tablespoons self-
  raising flour

pinch salt
1 tablespoon hot water
½ teaspoon butter

Cheese Filling:

1 lb. packaged cream
  cheese
½ cup sugar
2 eggs
1½ teaspoons vanilla
1 dessertspoon grated
  lemon rind
1½ tablespoons
  lemon juice

1 tablespoon gelatine
½ cup water
½ pint sour cream
2 tablespoons brandy
¼ pint cream
1 oz. slivered almonds
1 oz. dark chocolate

Sponge Layer: Beat egg-white until stiff, gradually add sugar, beating well after each addition; beat in egg-yolk. Lightly fold in sifted dry ingredients. Add combined water and butter; mix thoroughly. Pour mixture into greased 8 in. sandwich tin.

Bake in moderate oven 12 to 15 minutes. Turn out on to cake rack, allow to cool.

When cold, place in 8 in, springform pan which has been lightly greased round sides and base lined with greaseproof paper.

Cheese Filling: Beat cheese until smooth. Beat eggs and sugar until light and fluffy, beat into softened cheese. Stir in sour cream, lemon juice and rind, vanilla, and brandy. Soften gelatine in the water, dissolve over hot water.

Add to cheese mixture. Pour on top of sponge layer, refrigerate overnight.

Before serving, spread top of cheesecake with whipped cream, sprinkle over toasted almonds, drizzle with melted chocolate.

Note: Make cheesecake the day before it is to be served and refrigerate overnight. Instead of making sponge cake layer, 8 in. sponge cake layer can be bought; cut it in half, horizontally. Use only one layer for base of cheesecake. The remaining half can be frozen for later use.

Brandied-Crumb Cheesecake

Crumb Crust:

6 oz. plain sweet
  biscuits
1 oz. ground almonds
¼ cup icing sugar

3 oz. butter
½ teaspoon cinnamon
1½ tablespoons brandy

Filling:

1½ tablespoons
  gelatine
¼ cup cold water
2 eggs, separated
⅔ cup milk

1 cup sugar
pinch salt
1 lb. cottage cheese
1 tablespoon lemon juice
1 tablespoon brandy
½ pint cream

Crumb Crust: Crush biscuits. Combine crushed biscuits, melted butter and all remaining ingredients. Press crumbs evenly over base of greased 8 in. springform pan.

Refrigerate until firm.

Lemon-Meringue Cake—tangy lemon filling needs no baking (See page 38).

Filling: Soften gelatine in cold water. Combine egg-yolks, milk, sugar and salt in saucepan.

Stir over low heat until custard thickens slightly.

While still hot, dissolve gelatine mixture in this; cool. Sieve cheese. Beat together cheese, lemon juice, and brandy until smooth. Beat in egg-yolk mixture. Beat egg-whites until soft and fold into cheese mixture together with whipped cream.

Pour on to prepared crumb crust.

Refrigerate until set.

Cherry Cheese Tart

Crumb Case:

6 oz. plain sweet biscuits   3 oz. butter
2 tablespoons icing sugar

Filling:

8 oz. cream cheese   2 tablespoons lemon
½ cup sweetened   juice
  condensed milk   ¼ pint cream

Topping:

¾ lb. cherries   1 tablespoon arrowroot
1 cup water   few drops red food
2 tablespoons sugar   colouring

Crumb Case: Crush biscuits to fine crumbs, combine with sifted icing sugar and melted butter. Press on to base and sides of 9 in. pie plate.

Refrigerate while preparing filling.

Filling: Sieve cream cheese, add condensed milk and lemon juice; beat until smooth. Fold in whipped cream.

Pour into prepared pie case.

Refrigerate several hours.

Topping: Combine washed, stemmed cherries with sugar and water; cook gently until cherries are slightly softened; remove from pan and, when cool, arrange decoratively on top of cream cheese mixture.

Blend arrowroot in little water, add to syrup in saucepan; cook, stirring, until thickened. Add a few drops of red food colouring to give a bright colour. Spoon over cherries.

Refrigerate until glaze has set.

Note: When cherries are out of season, topping can be made with canned cherries. Drain cherries, arrange on top of pie. Thicken 1 cup cherry syrup with 1 tablespoon arrowroot blended in a little water. Cook, stirring, until thickened. Spoon over cherries.

Strawberry Cheese Tart

Omit cherry topping. Whip ¼ pint cream, pipe decorative edge around edge of tart. Fill inside the cream border with halved fresh strawberries; spoon over bottled strawberry topping to cover the strawberries and top of tart.

Note: In place of pie dish, 8 in. springform pan can be used. Use only 4 oz. crushed biscuits, 1 tablespoon icing sugar and 2 oz. melted butter; press over base only of 8 in. springform pan.

Caramel-Topped Cheesecake

Crumb Crust:

6 oz. plain sweet   3 oz. butter
  biscuits

Cream Layer:

1 dessertspoon gelatine   3 tablespoons sugar
¼ cup water   3 egg-yolks
8 oz. packaged   ¼ cup lemon juice
  cream cheese

Caramel Topping:

1 oz. butter   ¼ cup cold water
2 tablespoons brown   1 dessertspoon golden
  sugar   syrup
2 tablespoons   4 tablespoons hot water
  sweetened   2 teaspoons gelatine
  condensed milk

Crumb Crust: Crush biscuits finely, add melted butter; combine well. Press over base and sides of greased 7 in. sandwich tin with removable base.

Refrigerate.

Cream Layer: Soften gelatine in water, dissolve over hot water. Beat cream cheese until smooth, gradually add sugar, beat well. Add egg-yolks, lemon juice, and dissolved gelatine. Spoon filling evenly into crumb crust.

Refrigerate until set.

Pour cooled caramel over top of cream layer, refrigerate again to set caramel.

Caramel Topping: Soften gelatine in ¼ cup cold water, allow to stand. Combine in saucepan butter, brown sugar, condensed milk, and golden syrup. Cook, stirring constantly, until mixture is rich golden colour and leaves sides of saucepan.

Remove from heat, gradually stir in hot water. Return to heat, cook further 1 to 2 minutes, stir in softened gelatine; allow to cool.

Chestnut Cheesecake

Crumb Base:

6 oz. plain sweet biscuits	3 oz. butter

Filling:

8 oz. packaged cream cheese	2 tablespoons lemon juice
16 oz. can chestnut puree	1 teaspoon vinegar
½ cup sweetened condensed milk	½ cup cream
	2 teaspoons rum

Crumb Base: Crush biscuits finely, push through sieve, add melted butter; combine well. Press over base of 8 in. springform pan.

Filling: Remove chestnut puree from can, divide in two equal parts; reserve one part for topping. Sieve remaining puree, beat with the cream cheese; add condensed milk, lemon juice, vinegar. Beat until mixture is richly creamy.

Fold in whipped cream and rum. Pour over prepared crumb base.

Refrigerate.

When filling is firm, smooth desired topping over (see below), refrigerate again until topping has firmed.

You might like to serve a bowl of whipped cream separately.

We have given a choice of two toppings—the first is like a rich chestnut mousse; the second retains more of the true chestnut flavour. But they're equally delicious!

Topping No. 1:

2 oz. butter	2 tablespoons boiling water
¼ cup castor sugar	
chestnut puree	1 tablespoon rum
2 oz. dark chocolate	

Cream butter and sugar until white and fluffy; sieve reserved chestnut puree, add to butter mixture, beat well. Melt finely chopped chocolate in the hot water, add to creamed mixture, beat well; beat in rum. Spread on top of cheesecake.

Refrigerate until firm.

Topping No. 2:

¼ cup water	1 tablespoon cream
⅔ cup sugar	1 teaspoon rum
chestnut puree	

Make a syrup by placing water and sugar into heavy saucepan, bring slowly to boil, stirring constantly. When all sugar has dissolved, boil rapidly without stirring until syrup forms soft ball when a little is dropped into glass of cold water. Blend syrup into reserved sieved chestnut puree, beat well. Add cream and rum, beat until smooth.
Note: There are two types of canned chestnuts; one is pureed chestnuts flavoured with sugar, glucose and vanilla. The other is pure chestnuts pureed; the second type should be used in above recipe. Check ingredients on can.

Chocolate Cheesecake

Crumb Crust:

4 oz. plain chocolate biscuits	2 oz. melted butter

Filling:

8 oz. packaged cream cheese	2 eggs, separated
½ cup sugar	1 cup cream
1 teaspoon vanilla	4 oz. dark chocolate
	pinch salt
	+gelatine

Crumb Crust: Combine crushed biscuit crumbs and melted butter, mix well. Press mixture on to base of greased 8 in. springform pan.

Filling: Beat cheese until smooth, add ¼ cup sugar and the vanilla, beat well. Add lightly beaten egg-yolks and chocolate, which has been melted over hot water.

Beat egg-whites and salt until peaks form, gradually beat in remaining sugar; fold into chocolate mixture. Finally, fold through the whipped cream.

Refrigerate until set.

To serve, decorate with extra whipped cream and grated chocolate.

Classic Cheesecake

1 lb. packaged cream cheese	½ pint sour cream
½ cup sugar	2 teaspoons vanilla
3 egg-yolks	1 tablespoon gelatine
3 tablespoons condensed milk	4 tablespoons water
⅓ cup lemon juice	whipped cream
	8 in. crumb crust

Beat cheese until smooth. Beat egg-yolks and sugar until light and fluffy, add to softened cheese. Stir in sour cream, condensed milk, lemon juice, and vanilla, mix well. Soften gelatine in water, dissolve over hot water, cool; add to cheese mixture. Pour into prepared crumb crust.

Refrigerate until set.

Serve topped with whipped cream.

Citrus Cheesecake

Crumb Crust:

6 oz. plain sweet biscuits	½ teaspoon nutmeg
3 oz. butter	

Filling:

1 tablespoon gelatine	3 tablespoons lemon juice
¼ cup water	3 tablespoons orange juice
2 eggs, separated	1 dessertspoon grated lemon rind
½ teaspoon salt	1 lb. cream cheese
½ cup milk	1 teaspoon vanilla
½ cup sugar	1 cup cream
½ cup brown sugar	

Crumb Crust: Crush biscuits, add nutmeg and melted butter; mix well. Press mixture firmly round sides and base of well-greased 7 in. pan with removable base.

Filling: Soften gelatine in water, stand 5 minutes. Beat egg-yolks, salt, and milk, place in top of double boiler and cook over hot water until thickened, stirring constantly. Remove from heat, add white and brown sugars, stir until sugars dissolve.

Add orange and lemon juices and lemon rind. Stir in gelatine.

Cool until beginning to thicken. Beat in sieved cream cheese and vanilla until smooth. Fold in softly beaten egg-whites alternately with whipped cream.

Spread filling evenly into crumb crust.

Refrigerate overnight or at least 6 hours. Before serving decorate with extra whipped cream.

Cream Cheesecake

8 oz. packaged cream cheese	¼ cup water
½ cup sugar	¼ cup lemon juice
¼ cup milk	¼ cup sugar, extra
1 tablespoon gelatine	1 teaspoon grated lemon rind
3 eggs	8 in. crumb crust

Separate eggs. Soften cheese in top of double saucepan with sugar, add milk and lightly beaten egg-yolks; stir constantly over hot water 15 minutes or until thickened slightly. Soften gelatine in cold water, add lemon juice.

Remove cheese mixture from heat, stir in gelatine mixture; cool. Beat egg-whites until stiff, gradually add extra sugar. Fold into cheese mixture together with lemon rind, pour into crumb crust.

Refrigerate until set.

Serve with whipped cream or fresh or canned fruit.

Coffee-Cream Cheesecake

4 oz. cottage cheese	1 tablespoon grated lemon rind
12 oz. cream cheese	1 tablespoon lemon juice
1 tablespoon gelatine	1 tablespoon instant coffee powder
3 tablespoons cold water	1 egg-white
2 tablespoons boiling water	¾ cup sugar
½ pint cream	8 in. crumb crust

Sieve cheeses into a bowl, beat well. Soften gelatine in cold water, add boiling water, stir until dissolved; add instant coffee. Add to cheese mixture with lemon rind and juice, continue beating until smooth. Whip cream until stiff.

Beat egg-white, gradually add sugar, continue beating until meringue consistency. Fold whipped cream, then egg-white carefully into cheese mixture. Pour into prepared crumb crust.

Refrigerate several hours or until set.

If desired, decorate top, just before serving, with grated chocolate.

Coffee Cheesecake

Crumb Crust:

5 oz. plain sweet biscuits	1 teaspoon cinnamon
2 tablespoons powdered milk	3 oz. butter

Filling:

1 lb. cottage cheese	2 eggs
½ cup brown sugar	4 oz. can reduced cream
1 tablespoon instant coffee powder	1 tablespoon gelatine
1 teaspoon vanilla	2 tablespoons water
	¼ cup brown sugar, extra

Crumb Crust: Crush biscuits, add powdered milk and cinnamon. Melt butter and add to dry ingredients, mix well. Press crumb mixture on to base of 8 in. springform pan.

Refrigerate.

Filling: Separate eggs. Sieve cottage cheese. Soften gelatine in the water, dissolve over hot water. Add ½ cup brown sugar, coffee, vanilla, egg-yolks, reduced cream, and gelatine; beat thoroughly. Whip egg-whites, gradually beat in extra brown sugar, fold through coffee mixture. Pour into crumb crust.

Refrigerate until set.

Serve with whipped cream, sprinkled with cinnamon.

Mocha Cheesecake, and the true mocha flavour is in both the crumb crust and the delicious filling (page 40)

Coffee Liqueur Cheesecake

Crumb Crust:

8 oz. coconut biscuits	4 oz. butter

Filling:

8 oz. cottage cheese	½ pint cream
8 oz. packaged cream cheese	1 teaspoon grated lemon rind
2 egg whites	¼ cup lemon juice
½ cup sugar	3 tablespoons coffee liqueur
1 dessertspoon gelatine	
2 tablespoons cold water	2 oz. melted chocolate

Crumb Crust: Crush biscuits into crumbs or put through electric blender. Mix in melted butter, blend well. Press mixture on to base and sides of 8 in. springform pan.

Refrigerate while preparing filling.

Filling: Push cottage cheese through sieve, combine in a mixing bowl with cream cheese; beat together well. Soften gelatine in cold water, dissolve over hot water.

Add to creamed mixture with lemon rind and juice, continue beating until smooth. Beat in coffee liqueur.

Beat egg-whites, gradually add sugar, continue beating until stiff. Fold whipped cream, then egg-whites carefully into creamed mixture.

Pour into prepared crumb crust.

Refrigerate 6 hours or overnight.

Before serving, drizzle melted chocolate over the surface of cheesecake.

Fruit Salad Cheesecake

⅔ cup lemonade	1 dessertspoon lemon juice
½ cup sugar	
1 tablespoon gelatine	1 teaspoon vanilla
12 oz. packaged cream cheese	1 cup cream
	15 oz. can fruit salad
1 tablespoon grated lemon rind	8 in. crumb crust

Combine lemonade, sugar, and gelatine in saucepan, stir over medium heat until gelatine and sugar are dissolved.

Cool.

Cream cheese, lemon rind, lemon juice and vanilla, beat in cooled gelatine mixture. Refrigerate until partly set. Fold in whipped cream and well-drained fruit salad. Pour into prepared crumb crust.

Refrigerate until set.

Creamy Coffee Cheesecake

Crumb Crust:

6 oz. coconut biscuits	3 oz. butter

Filling:

¾ cup sugar	1 tablespoon instant coffee powder
1 tablespoon gelatine	
¼ teaspoon salt	1 lb. cream cheese
2 eggs	1 teaspoon vanilla
1 cup milk	¼ cup sugar, extra
¼ pint cream	

Coffee Cream:

¼ pint cream	1 teaspoon sugar
1 teaspoon instant coffee powder	

Crumb Crust: Crush biscuits, add melted butter; blend well. Press on to base of greased 8 in. springform pan.

Refrigerate.

Filling: Separate eggs. Combine sugar, gelatine, and salt. Add beaten egg-yolks and milk; blend well.

Place in top of double saucepan, stir over hot water until gelatine dissolves. Remove from heat, stir in coffee powder; cool. Sieve cream cheese, beat until smooth; stir into gelatine mixture with vanilla.

Refrigerate, stirring occasionally until creamy and smooth.

Beat egg-whites to soft peaks; gradually add extra sugar, beating to stiff peaks. Fold into gelatine mixture, then fold in whipped cream until mixture becomes smooth. Pour on to prepared crumb crust; refrigerate until set. Spread whipped Coffee Cream over top, sprinkle with grated chocolate.

Coffee Cream: Combine all ingredients, refrigerate ½ hour. When ready to use, beat until thick.

Ginger Cheesecake

Crumb Crust:

10 oz. plain sweet biscuits	3 oz. dark chocolate
5 oz. butter	1 teaspoon ground ginger

Filling:

1 lb. packaged cream cheese	1 dessertspoon ginger syrup
½ cup brown sugar	1 tablespoon gelatine
2 egg yolks	3 tablespoons water
1½ tablespoons rum	1 cup evaporated milk
2 tablespoons chopped preserved ginger	

Topping:

2 egg whites	1 dessertspoon rum
1 tablespoon sugar	1 tablespoon chopped preserved ginger
½ pint cream	

Crumb Crust: Crush biscuits, melt butter with chopped chocolate over low heat. Add ginger and melted ingredients to biscuit crumbs. Press over base and sides of 9 in. springform pan; refrigerate.

Filling: Beat cream cheese and brown sugar until smooth. Add egg-yolks, beat well. Add rum, ginger and syrup. Soften gelatine in water, dissolve over hot water.

Beat well-chilled evaporated milk until thick, beat in dissolved gelatine. Fold through cheese mixture. Whip egg-whites until stiff, fold in.

Pour into crumb case; refrigerate.

Topping: Whip egg-whites, gradually beat in sugar; beat well. Whip cream, beat in rum, carefully fold in ginger and beaten egg-whites.

Spread over filling, drizzle 1 oz. melted chocolate decoratively across top.

Jelly Cheesecake

1 pkt. lemon jelly	½ cup lemon juice
14 oz. can sweetened condensed milk	1 teaspoon grated lemon rind
1 teaspoon vanilla	8 oz. packaged cream cheese
4 tablespoons boiling water	8 in. crumb crust

Dissolve lemon jelly in boiling water, add lemon juice and rind; cool. Whip milk until thick. Beat cream cheese until soft, gradually add milk, vanilla, and jelly, beat well. Pour into crumb case.

Refrigerate until set.

Grapefruit Cheesecake

Crumb Crust:

8 oz. plain sweet biscuits	¼ teaspoon cinnamon
¼ teaspoon nutmeg	4 oz. butter

Filling:

2 to 3 large grapefruit	¼ cup cold water
½ teaspoon grated grapefruit rind	1 dessertspoon lemon juice
½ cup grapefruit juice	½ teaspoon grated lemon rind
2 eggs	1 lb. cream cheese
¾ cup sugar	½ cup cream
pinch salt	
1 tablespoon gelatine	

Crumb Crust: Crush biscuits very finely, blend with the nutmeg and cinnamon. Add melted butter, mix well. Press over base and sides of 8 in. springform pan.

Refrigerate while preparing filling.

Filling: Peel grapefruit, removing all white pith and membrane. Section the fruit; do this over a bowl so no juice is lost. Squeeze the juice from the membrane; there should be about ½ cup altogether. Set aside 6 or 8 nice grapefruit sections for decoration, cut remainder into small pieces.

Separate 1 egg. In top of double boiler beat together the yolk, plus 1 whole egg, the sugar, salt, and 1 tablespoon of grapefruit juice.

Cook over gently boiling water, stirring until smoothly thickened. Soften gelatine in ¼ cup cold water. Stir into cooked custard until dissolved.

Remove from heat, cool.

Press cream cheese through fine sieve, blend thoroughly with remaining grapefruit juice, fruit rinds and juice. Beat gradually into cooled custard.

Fold grapefruit pieces, softly whipped cream, and softly beaten egg-white into cheese mixture. Spoon into prepared crumb crust, decorate with grapefruit sections.

Refrigerate several hours or overnight.

Lemon Cheesecake

1 lb. cream cheese	2 teaspoons vinegar
1 cup sweetened condensed milk	1 cup cream
⅓rd cup lemon juice	extra cream
	8 in. crumb crust

Sieve cream cheese, add condensed milk, lemon juice, and vinegar. Beat until mixture is creamy. Fold whipped cream into cheese mixture.

Pour into crumb crust; refrigerate overnight. Top with extra whipped cream, sprinkle with nutmeg.

Lemon Jelly Cheesecake

Sponge Layer:

1 egg
2 tablespoons
castor sugar
3½ tablespoons
self-raising flour

pinch salt
1 tablespoon hot water
½ teaspoon butter

Filling:

8 oz. cream cheese
¾ cup evaporated milk
¼ cup lemon juice
¼ cup sugar

½ packet lemon jelly
crystals
½ cup boiling water

Sponge Layer: Separate egg. Beat egg-white until stiff, gradually add sugar, beating well after each addition; beat in egg-yolk. Lightly fold in sifted dry ingredients. Add combined water and butter; mix thoroughly. Pour mixture into greased 8 in. sandwich tin. Bake in moderate oven 12 to 15 minutes. Turn out on to cake rack, allow to cool. When cold, place in 8 in. springform pan which has been lightly greased round sides and base lined with greaseproof paper.

Filling: Dissolve jelly crystals and sugar in boiling water, add lemon juice; cool slightly. Push cream cheese through sieve, then beat until soft.

Gradually beat in jelly mixture. Beat well-chilled evaporated milk until thick; fold in jelly mixture. Pour over sponge cake layer.

Refrigerate several hours until firm.

Lemon-Meringue Cake

Crumb Crust:

½ lb. plain sweet
biscuits

4 oz. butter

Filling:

8 oz. pkt. cream cheese
14 oz. can sweetened
condensed milk
2 eggs, separated

1 dessertspoon grated
lemon rind
¼ cup lemon juice
½ cup castor sugar

Crumb Crust: Crush biscuits, mix in melted butter; press into 8 in. springform pan, lining base and bringing crumb mixture ¾ of way up sides.

Filling: Beat cheese until smooth, beat in condensed milk, lemon rind and juice, and egg-yolks; pour into prepared crumb crust.

Whip whites until soft, gradually beat in half the sugar, beat until stiff, fold in remaining sugar. Spread evenly over filling.

Bake in hot oven 10 minutes to brown the meringue.

Remove from tin when cold.

Tangy Lemon Cheesecake

Crumb Crust:

6 oz. coconut biscuits
3 oz. melted butter
1½ tablespoons sugar
½ teaspoon nutmeg

1 teaspoon grated
lemon rind
½ cup finely chopped
walnuts
½ teaspoon cinnamon

Filling:

8 oz. packaged
cream cheese
½ cup sweetened
condensed milk

2 tablespoons lemon
juice
1 teaspoon grated
lemon rind
½ cup cream

Topping:

1 oz. butter
½ cup sugar

1 egg
1 tablespoon lemon juice

Crumb Crust: Mix all ingredients together in basin; blend well, press into 9 in. pie plate.

Refrigerate while preparing filling.

Filling: Beat together cream cheese, condensed milk, lemon juice, rind; beat until smooth. Fold in whipped cream. Spoon into pie case, smooth top.

Refrigerate.

Topping: Melt butter. Beat together sugar, egg, and lemon juice. Put into small saucepan with butter, cook over hot water, stirring constantly, until the mixture thickens. Cool, pour over pie.

Frozen Marsala Cheesecake

This is an entirely new type of cheesecake which is firmed in the freezing compartment of the refrigerator. It makes a superb dessert.

5 egg-yolks
½ cup sugar
¾ cup marsala
8 oz. packaged cream
cheese

1 oz. butter
30 oz. carton vanilla
ice-cream
2 oz. plain sweet biscuit
crumbs

Melt butter, add crumbs, and mix well. Press on to base of greased 8 in. springform pan.

Place egg-yolks and sugar into top of double boiler, beat until thick; add marsala, whisk over gently simmering water until mixture thickens slightly.

Remove from heat, allow to cool.

Beat cream cheese until soft and smooth, gradually beat in cooled mixture. Lastly, fold in softened ice-cream.

Pour on to prepared base, freeze overnight, or for several hours, until firm.

Pineapple-Topped Cheesecake (See page 41).

biscuits with melted butter; blend well. Reserve ¼ cup biscuit mixture for topping.

Press remainder on base and sides of 8 in. springform pan.

Filling: Dissolve jelly in boiling water, add white wine; refrigerate until slightly thickened. Beat cheese and orange juice together until creamy.

Add jelly and beat further 3 minutes; fold in whipped cream. Pour mixture in to prepared crumb crust. Sprinkle with remaining ¼ cup crumb mixture.

Refrigerate several hours or overnight.

Port Wine Cheesecake

Use port wine or strawberry jelly instead of pineapple jelly in previous recipe, and replace the white wine with port wine. This makes an unusual wine-flavoured cheesecake, light pink in colour.

Pineapple-Topped Cheesecake

Base:

4 oz. shortbread biscuits
1½ oz. butter

¼ cup finely chopped almonds

Cheesecake Filling:

¼ cup lemon juice
1 dessertspoon grated lemon rind
8 oz. packaged cream cheese
1 cup sugar

2 eggs, separated
1 tablespoon gelatine
3 tablespoons water
½ pint cream

Pineapple Topping:

¼ cup lemon juice
1 dessertspoon grated lemon rind
½ pkt. lemon jelly crystals
½ cup hot water

1 tablespoon dry vermouth or white wine
¾ cup canned crushed pineapple

Base: Grease 8 in. springform pan, line base and sides with greased greaseproof paper. Crush biscuits finely. Melt butter in saucepan, add nuts. Fry gently until golden, remove from heat; add biscuit crumbs, mix well. Press evenly over base of prepared tin.

Filling: Beat cream cheese and sugar until smooth, add lemon rind and juice, beat to combine; add egg-yolks, beat 2 minutes.

Soften gelatine in the water, dissolve over hot water, cool slightly, beat into cheese mixture. Whip cream; beat egg-whites until soft peaks form. Fold cream into cheese mixture very carefully, then fold in egg-whites. Spoon carefully into tin over prepared base.

Refrigerate until firm.

Pineapple Topping: Dissolve jelly in the hot water, add juice and rind of lemon, and vermouth. Stir in undrained pineapple, Refrigerate until on point of setting. Spoon carefully over cheesecake.

Refrigerate several hours or overnight.

Remove from tin, carefully peel off the paper.

Pineapple Cheesecake

Crumb Crust:

3 oz. plain sweet biscuits
2 oz. melted butter
1 tablespoon sugar

¼ cup chopped nuts
¼ teaspoon cinnamon
¼ teaspoon nutmeg

Filling:

¾ cup sugar
1 tablespoon gelatine
¼ teaspoon salt
2 eggs
½ cup evaporated milk
1 teaspoon grated lemon rind

8 oz. cream cheese
1 tablespoon lemon juice
1 teaspoon vanilla
¼ cup sugar, extra
¼ pint cream
15 oz. can crushed pineapple

Crumb Crust: Crush biscuits finely. Mix together all crumb crust ingredients, line base of 8 in. springform pan with the mixture.

Filling: Separate eggs. Combine in top of double saucepan the sugar, gelatine, salt, beaten egg-yolks, evaporated milk.

Cook over simmering water, stirring constantly until gelatine is dissolved and mixture thickens slightly (approximately 10 minutes). Add grated lemon rind; cool. Press cheese through strainer, stir in lemon juice and vanilla, blend with first mixture.

Refrigerate, stirring occasionally, until mixture is partially set. Beat egg-whites until peaks form; gradually add extra ¼ cup sugar, beating until sugar is dissolved and egg-whites are stiff. Fold into gelatine mixture. Beat cream until thick, fold in cream, then drained crushed pineapple. Pour mixture over crumb crust.

Refrigerate until filling is firm.

Rum Cheesecake

Crumb Crust:

3 oz. plain sweet biscuits	1 tablespoon sugar
¼ teaspoon cinnamon	2 oz. butter
¼ teaspoon nutmeg	¼ cup almonds, finely chopped

Filling:

1 tablespoon gelatine	1 cup milk
1 cup sugar	1 tablespoon lemon juice
¼ teaspoon salt	2 tablespoons rum
2 eggs	1½ lb. cream cheese
1 teaspoon grated lemon rind	1 cup cream

Crumb Crust: Crush biscuits finely. Melt butter, add almonds, and brown lightly; do not burn. Add to dry ingredients, mix well. Sprinkle half crumb mixture on base of greased 8 in. springform pan, press on firmly; reserve remainder.

Filling: Separate eggs. Mix gelatine, ¾ cup sugar, and salt in top of double saucepan, beat in egg-yolks and milk. Stir over hot water until gelatine dissolves and mixture thickens (approx. 10 min.)

Add lemon rind, juice and rum; cool. Sieve cream cheese, beat until smooth, stir in cooled gelatine mixture.

Beat egg-whites until stiff but not dry. Gradually add remaining sugar, beat until very stiff. Fold into custard mixture; fold in whipped cream. Pour into prepared springform pan, sprinkle with reserved nut-crumb mixture. Smooth over with back of spoon.

Refrigerate overnight.

Strawberry Cheesecake

Crumb Crust:

4 oz. butter	8 oz. plain sweet biscuits
2 tablespoons castor sugar	2 teaspoons cinnamon

Filling:

1 tablespoon gelatine	1 dessertspoon grated lemon rind
1 cup cold water	¼ teaspoon salt
3 eggs	1 cup cream
½ cup sugar	1 cup halved strawberries
1 lb. cream cheese	1 tablespoon brandy
2 tablespoons lemon juice	extra whole strawberries
	2 tablespoons red currant jelly

Crumb Crust: Crush biscuits, add melted butter, sugar and cinnamon; stir well. Line base and sides of 8 in. springform pan with crumb mixture.

Refrigerate while preparing filling.

Cover halved strawberries with brandy and set aside; stir occasionally.

Filling: Press cheese through coarse sieve. Soften gelatine in ½ cup water. Separate eggs, put beaten yolks, sugar, and remaining ½ cup water into double boiler, cook over hot water, stirring, until thickened.

Add soaked gelatine, stir to dissolve in hot mixture; strain into cheese, beat well until smooth and creamy; add lemon rind, juice, and salt.

Refrigerate until beginning to thicken. Whip cream lightly, add to mixture with softly beaten egg-whites. Lastly, fold in brandied strawberries; be careful not to crush berries.

Pour mixture into prepared crumb crust, refrigerate 6 hours, or overnight. Before serving arrange extra strawberries round edge of cheesecake, glaze them with warmed red currant jelly.

Yoghurt Cheesecake

Crumb Crust:

10 oz. sweet plain biscuits	¼ teaspoon cinnamon
5 oz. butter	

Filling:

1½ tablespoons gelatine	¾ cup sugar
½ cup cold water	pinch salt
1 lb. cottage cheese	1 tablespoon grated lemon rind
1 cup yoghurt	1 tablespoon lemon juice
4 eggs	½ cup sugar, extra
	1 cup cream

Crumb Crust: Crush biscuits finely, push through strainer, mix with cinnamon. Add melted butter, blend well. Press mixture over base and sides of 9 in. springform pan.

Refrigerate 1 hour.

Filling: Soften gelatine in cold water. Push cottage cheese through sieve, beat with yoghurt until smooth. Separate eggs. In top of double boiler, beat yolks with sugar, salt, and lemon rind until thick and lemon-coloured.

Cook over hot water, stirring constantly, 5 minutes. Add softened gelatine, stir until dissolved.

Cool slightly, stir in lemon juice, then add yoghurt-cheese mixture. Beat egg-whites until stiff, gradually add sugar, continue beating until meringue consistency. Fold in lemon mixture, then fold in whipped cream. Pour carefully into prepared crumb crust.

Refrigerate at least 8 hours or overnight.

A delicious cheescake, specialty of the Wentworth Hotel, Sydney (see page 45).

From the Restaurants

Many Australian restaurants, well known for their excellent food, have made a specialty of cheesecakes. On this page we give, by permission of the restaurants concerned, some of these famous cheesecake recipes

Chevron Hotel, Sydney

1¼ lb. packaged cream cheese
½ cup castor sugar
2 eggs
2 tablespoons grated lemon rind
⅓ cup cream
8 in. crumb crust

Beat together cream cheese and sugar until smooth; beat in eggs 1 at a time, beat on electric mixer at medium speed 10 minutes; beat in lemon rind and cream, beat to blend.

Pour into crumb crust, bake in moderately slow oven 20 minutes, reduce heat to slow, bake further 40 minutes or until surface is firm to touch.

Menzies Hotel, Sydney

1¾ lb. packaged cream cheese
¾ cup sugar
3 eggs
2 oz. sultanas
½ teaspoon lemon essence
½ teaspoon vanilla
8 in. crumb crust

Spread sultanas evenly over base of crumb crust. Beat cream cheese until smooth, gradually beat in sugar. Add eggs, one at a time, beating well, add essences; spoon into crumb crust. Bake in slow oven 1 hour. Cool, then refrigerate.

Fanny's Restaurant, Melbourne

Crumb Crust:

3 oz. unsalted butter
2 oz. plain biscuits
1 tablespoon castor sugar
1 teaspoon cinnamon
2 oz. ground walnuts

Filling:

1 lb. packaged cream cheese
1 oz. unsalted butter
¾ cup castor sugar
3 eggs, separated
1 dessertspoon finely-chopped lemon rind
½ pint sour cream
1 teaspoon vanilla
3 tablespoons plain flour
1 dessertspoon strained lemon juice

Crumb Crust: Melt butter over low heat, brush base and sides of 9 in. springform pan thickly with some of the butter. Crush biscuits finely, add to remaining butter with sugar, cinnamon and walnuts; mix well. Press mixture over base and sides of prepared pan. Crumb crust will be thin. Refrigerate while preparing filling.

Filling: Beat cream cheese and butter until smooth and creamy, add sugar and egg-yolks; beat well. Add sour cream, vanilla and sifted flour; beat until smooth, beat in lemon rind and juice. Beat egg-whites until soft peaks form, fold lightly into cream cheese mixture. Pour into prepared pan, stand on baking tray, bake in slow oven approximately 1½ hours or until firm to touch. Cool in oven with door ajar.

The Rhine Castle Bistro, Sydney

Crumb Crust:

8 oz. plain sweet biscuits

4 oz. butter

Filling:

1½ lb. packaged cream cheese
1 cup sugar

2 eggs
1 teaspoon vanilla
whipped cream

Crumb Crust: Crush the biscuits into fine crumbs, melt butter, add to crumbs, mix well. Line 8 in. springform pan.

Filling: Cream the cheese and sugar together, add eggs one at a time, then add vanilla, and beat well. Pour mixture into the crumb crust. Bake 30 minutes in a slow oven. Leave in the oven until cool. Refrigerate at least 2 hours (overnight is better still).

When ready to serve, top with sweetened whipped cream and sprinkle with nutmeg.

The Summit Restaurant, Sydney

1 lb. cottage cheese
¾ cup sugar
3 egg-yolks
1 tablespoon gelatine
2 tablespoons water
¼ cup lemon juice

1 dessertspoon grated lemon rind
1 small can mandarin segments
1 pint cream
8 in. sponge cake layer

Carefully cut away one-third of the sponge cake layer and place at base of 8 in. springform pan. (Remaining sponge can be used for another dessert.)

Beat cheese well to soften, gradually beat in sugar and egg-yolks. Soften gelatine in the water, dissolve over hot water, mix in to cheese mixture. Add lemon rind and juice. Chop 1 tablespoon of the drained mandarin segments, mix into cream cheese; blend in whipped cream. Carefully spoon over sponge cake layer. Refrigerate until firm.

Decorate with remaining mandarin segments and whipped cream.

Wentworth Hotel, Sydney

There is a thin layer of sponge cake on the base and on top of this beautiful cheesecake. It can be a 6, 7, or 8 in. sponge, depending on the size of the springform pan in which it will set. Naturally, if you use the larger size, the cake will not be so tall.

Cut 2 slices off the sponge cake layer, approximately ¼ in. thick.

10 oz. packaged cream cheese
¾ cup sugar
4 eggs
1 tablespoon lemon juice
1½ tablespoons gelatine

½ pint cream
2 tablespoons cold water
icing sugar
1 sponge cake layer

Beat together cream cheese and sugar in bowl 5 minutes. Add eggs, 1 at a time, beating well after each addition. Soak gelatine in cold water, dissolve in hot lemon juice, cool. Add gelatine mixture to cheese mixture, blend well. Fold in whipped cream. Line spring-form pan with greaseproof paper with paper extending 1 in. above tin. Place 1 sponge cake layer on base of prepared tin. Pour in cheese mixture. Top with other sponge layer. Sprinkle generously with sifted icing sugar. Refrigerate several hours or overnight.

Ye Old Crusty Cellar, Sydney

1½ lb. packaged cream cheese
4 egg-yolks
14 oz. can condensed milk
1 dessertspoon grated lemon rind

¼ cup lemon juice
1 tablespoon sugar
½ pint sour cream
1 tablespoon gelatine
1 cup warm water
9 in. crumb crust

Beat together for 15 minutes cream cheese, egg-yolks, condensed milk, lemon rind and juice, sugar, and sour cream. Add gelatine which has been dissolved in warm water; beat further 10 minutes. Pour into prepared crumb crust, refrigerate overnight.

Oven Temperatures

Gas

Very slow	250 deg. F.
Slow	275-300 deg. F.
Moderately slow	325 deg. F.
Moderate	350 deg. F.
Moderately hot	375 deg. F.
Hot	400-450 deg. F.
Very hot	475-500 deg. F.

Electric

Very slow	250 deg. F.
Slow	300 deg. F.
Moderately slow	325-350 deg. F.
Moderate	375-400 deg. F.
Moderately hot	425-450 deg. F.
Hot	475-500 deg. F.
Very hot	525-550 deg. F.